They Call Me Mama

What Happens When We Say Yes To God

Nicole Homan

Copyright 2021 by Nicole Homan

All rights reserved.

Printed in the United States of America.

ISBN: 9798737613945

Dedicated to my husband and children:

Jesus, you, then everything else.

Thank you for letting me share our story.

It's my favorite.

Contents

Introduction: 5

Chapter 1: Just Like He Said 8

Chapter 2: Finding Joy 21

Chapter 3: Facing My Greatest Fears 29

Chapter 4: The Birthday Gift 39

Chapter 5: Yes to Our Normal 48

Chapter 6: Yes to Intrusions 57

Chapter 7: Yes to the Unexpected 65

Chapter 8: Yes to Not Giving Up 73

Chapter 9: Yes to Redefining Everything 80

Chapter 10: Yes to Plowing and Waiting 89

Chapter 11: Yes to the Lessons 96

Chapter 12: Yes to Looking Up and Letting Go 105

Chapter 13: Yes to Deep-seeded Joy 112

Chapter 14: Yes to Giving Him Your Basket 120

Epilogue: 128

Introduction

I was going to be late. Quickening my pace, I followed the trail to the chapel where my mother was waiting to rehearse for evening service. At thirteen years of age, all middle school had offered me up to this point was heartbreak, acne, and the start of some seriously hairy legs. Here at summer camp, however, I was the daughter of the great "Pastor Carla Ives." Children swarmed around me, at the end of every service, asking for autographs and photos.

"Is it really the puppet talking or is it her?"

"You did such a good job dancing. Are you a real dancer?"

"I really like your hair. You are so pretty."

Everyone wanted to be my friend and everyone acted like we were friends. It was the best…or it would have been…if it had not been for the teenage counselors.

I had no idea how to process thoughts when they spoke to me. I often mumbled some inaudible Chewbacca-like noise as I looked at my feet in wonder—like I had never saw such remarkable scrunchy socks before. A few minutes of this and we'd both feel awkward. They were everything that intimidated me and everything that I wanted to be all rolled into one. How could one respond normally when standing before THAT?

When I finally reached the chapel, I realized that I had to go through the sea of campers and counselors who were already lining up, to enter the evening service. Locking eyes with my oversized Adidas shoes, I pressed through the crowd to the door. Maybe if I didn't look at them, they wouldn't speak to me.

And then…there he was, Matthew Scott Homan, the most good-looking boy I had ever seen not to mention three years my senior, holding the door open to the Chapel so I could enter. It was the Hallmark Movie moment of my dreams. I didn't even know his name, but he was an older boy and he opened the door for me – so did his name even matter? That's all I needed.

Before service began that night, I began planning our future. We'd be married in a few years and start a family in my twenties. Four, maybe five, children, sounded about right.

That night, I sang a song I wrote for the children of the camp. As I sang and poured my heart over the three chords I knew on piano, Matthew watched. Leaning over to his friend and fellow counselor, he whispered, "I think I'm going to marry a girl like that." And sure enough, he did.

Little did we know that the door that he opened for me that night would be the first of many doors he would open for me in the years to come.

Like the door of the church where we said our vows to one another in front of friends and family and the doors of the hospitals where I would waddle in holding my contracting belly and leave with a bundle of beauty in my arms. Like the doors to the DHS offices and adoption agencies where God would add to our family and the doors to the courthouses where we would hear the pound of that final gavel.

After fifteen years of marriage, fourteen children, and many, many doors…I can honestly say: Life has never been boring.

When we have asked the Lord, "What would you have us do? What is our purpose?" He has always responded with three simple words: "Live a yes."

"God, isn't there more?" we ask. "That seems so…simple."

"It's all I want," He replies over and over again. "Just live a yes."

And so that's what we've done. Our story has been written one faith-filled (and sometimes not as faith-filled) "Yes" at a time.

This book is my meager attempt at opening yet another door – but this time, it's for you. I want to share our lives with you—the good, the laughable, the hard, and the worth it. I want to give you more than a filtered Instagram picture or edited Facebook post. There is so much beauty and pain within every story—both significant, yet often lost when relegated to the caption underneath a simple photograph. This is what our "Yes" really looks like every single day. My prayer for you is that, as you read our story, you will find the courage to live YOUR "Yes" – whatever that might be.

So, come on in. Find a semi-clean chair and don't worry about wiping your feet. The rug is there for looks, not use – at least that's what my boys think.

Much Love,
Mama Bear

Chapter 1...
Just Like He Said

When Abe came, I became a Mama for the very first time. I still remember the first time I saw him—a picture on my computer screen. His big, brown eyes looked directly into my heart. I knew immediately he was to be our son—our first crazy, faith-filled "yes!" After waiting, for what seemed an eternity, for his photo to print from my computer, I rushed into my husband's office, slammed Abraham's photo on his desk, and joyfully exclaimed, "Meet your son!"

I will neither confirm nor deny if this was the correct way to introduce the idea of adoption and parenthood to my husband, but, thank the Lord Almighty, he gave me a man who loves my crazy and just rolls with it. Without missing a beat, he calmly asked, "Can you tell me more?" Oh, how I love that man.

By the end of the month, the process of adoption was well underway and our first letter to our son was being sent, the first of many. I'd love to say we handled the waiting months that followed with great patience. I'd love to say that we stood unwavering on the promises of God. But...that would be a lie. More often than not, I found myself consumed with doubt.

Did we miss God?

Would we have enough money?

Would he ever come home?

What if something went wrong?

What if we failed as parents?

We often say that it was Abraham who taught us what faith really looks like. Even in our doubts, even in our fears, even in our questions, God was faithful. As we continued to bring our fears to the Father, He quieted our every fear with a reminder of who He was, who He is. And with every reminder, we were infused with bravery and courage to take the next step of obedience and then the next and the next...even if our limbs shook underneath us.

Psalm 25:3 says, "Those who hope in You will not be put to shame." March 31, 2006, will forever be etched in my mind and heart as proof of the truth found within these words. That was the day when Abe came HOME.

I remember it like it was yesterday. I stood and waited nervously...breathlessly...impatiently for the doors of the airline to open and my baby to walk off that plane and into my arms. Joy and fear mixed into a bittersweet cocktail that was hard to swallow. Then, just when I began to question if they had missed their flight, the doors opened and there was my travel-weary husband holding the most beautiful two and half year old boy I had ever seen. All sound faded away around me except one…the sound of my father weeping from his place behind me. All of our prayers, all of the hours of paperwork, all of the travel, all of the extra jobs were worth it, in one-single-moment. I longed to hold him, smother him with kisses, never let him go. But to this beautiful boy, I was not yet known. I was foreign, a face from a photograph, a name on a letter addressed to him. Although my love was his for the taking, his love for me would have to be earned. And although my heart was already twined around his tiny fingers, his heart was guarded and unsure. Adoption had been given, now it had to be received. "Hello, Abe. I am your mommy." The words fumbled out of my dry mouth as the world stood still around us.

    Then, after what felt like the shortness of a breath and the length of eternity all in one, two tiny, brown arms reached for me. Not for forever, but for a moment. One beautiful, glorious, miraculous moment.

    The next morning, I woke to two dark eyes inspecting my freckled, pale face.

    "Good morning, Abraham."

    "Ugh," he nodded.

    "Are you ready to eat?" I quietly whispered, motioning with my hand any sign I could think of for "eat."

    "Ugh," he nodded again.

I got up, he followed, and that morning, he let me feed him breakfast, bathe him, read to him, dress him, play with him…just me and my boy. He let me in. And then it happened, "Mama," he said in all of his sweetness. "Mama," he said again, climbing up to sit next to me. "Yes, mama, Abe. I am mama."

Just like God promised.

Just like He said.

Looking back now, everything makes sense. They say hindsight is 20/20. We always look back and see things we missed…things we couldn't see when we were drowning in our heartache, lost in the oceanic current of our pain. Reasons why things happened the way they did become clearer, truth floats to the surface, and it all begins to make sense…after. This was my journey into motherhood.

I had prayed for a baby. For two years, I had waited and prayed and ate healthy and exercised. I can't remember how many tests I took, hoping, praying…only to fall on my knees on the bathroom floor, tears blurring that dreaded pink line screaming at me from the test stick. Oh, how I hated that line! It mocked me in my pain. Nothing had ever made me feel less of a woman than my inability to give my husband a child or more afraid that my dreams of family would be shattered by my own failure.

So, I stopped praying. I stopped hoping. I just…let go. As I laid to rest my dreams of carrying a child within me, God sent us Abraham. He was our miracle, the son of our hearts. I couldn't have been more thrilled or more in love. I was sure this was God's answer. Adoption had never been a "second choice" for us, it had always been a part of the dream. Since the day we drove home from our honeymoon and talked of the future, adoption had been on the table.

It all made sense. This was God's plan. I wouldn't even think about having a baby again. Abraham was my Isaac.

Joyfully, we prepared for his arrival. Paperwork complete, we busied ourselves with folding and refolding the massive assortment of outfits we had purchased for him, planning all the places we wanted to take him and all the things we wanted to do as a family. In those months, it felt like every day took 48 hours and every month held 60 days. Like an expectant mother yet with nothing to show for it, I carried around his photo, informing everyone I knew, and even those I didn't, that I would be a mother soon and that he was a boy. We tried to be patient. We didn't do a very good job of it. It was the final trimester, the last push…and I worried if we sat on the edge of our seats any longer, we might fall off.

Many nights were spent in Abe's room, holding on to the soft stuffed monkey we had made for him at Build-A-Bear, equal parts excited, impatient, and nervous. How could I love someone this deeply that I had never met? How could a stranger already feel so much a part of me? I sang lullabies into his empty room as I rocked in the chair that my mother used to rock me. I imagined my songs being carried on the wind, across the sea, and to his tiny ears. I pictured him wrapped in my love as a blanket, the melodies of each lullaby putting him to sleep, and I rocked and I rocked and rocked until the carpet underneath the chair had worn down…and yet still, we waited.

It was during those final months of waiting, that something out of the ordinary happened.

I, Nicole Homan, fell asleep…into a plate of lasagna. If you know me, you know that I love food—deeply, passionately, and profoundly—in all of its shapes and forms. To ruin a plate of good lasagna is an unthinkable travesty. I am disappointed in my younger self even now as I write this, but I just couldn't stay awake. Not on the family trip to Washington D.C., not as I stood on the lawn in front of the Washington Monument, not as I tried to carry on conversations with other humans, not even when we went to church.

"Niki," my mom whispered to me over a family meal, "I think you might be pregnant."

"No way!" I quickly replied. "It's not possible…is it?"

I couldn't even go there – I had closed that door. It hurt too bad to re-open it.

Weeks later, having forgotten about my conversation with my mother, I awoke at midnight with an intense craving for Burger King Whoppers. I had never experienced anything like this before and I immediately knew that if I did not eat a Whopper, I would die a painful and excruciating Whopper-less death. Knowing my husband would want to know this and remedy it as soon as possible, I shook him awake.

"Are you awake?" I asked, as he started to slap at my hands on his arm. This was a good sign.

"I need a whopper," I began, "Can you go get one for me?"

Turning over to look at me, obviously confused and not fully awake, he responded, "A whopper? No, Niki. They are closed." He then took hold of the sheet and proceeded to wrap himself back up and fall asleep. The nerve of that man.

"Matt, but I need one," I tried again, sure that if he had really heard me, he would have cared. "This is an emergency. Please, go get me a whopper."

Breathing a heavy sigh, he calmly but firmly reminded me once again that Burger King was not open and that he would not be going to get me a whopper. The audacity! I was appalled.

"Matt!" I cried, tears welling up in my eyes as heat rose in my cheeks, "I'm serious! I cannot go back to bed. I NEED one."

Sitting up and turning on the lamp beside the bed, my husband looked at me in bewilderment.

"Niki," he began stifling a yawn, "What do you want me to do? I can't get you a whopper."

"Yes, you can!" I demanded. "You can wake them up and tell them I need a whopper."

Rubbing his eyes and placing his glasses on his nose, Matt inspected me for a moment. It was as if he was searching for the place where the screw had finally come loose or for some explanation as to why his wife had become emotionally unstable over ground beef. Finding none, he again said, "Niki, I will not get you a whopper tonight."

You would think I would have accepted this final rejection, turned over, and fallen asleep. But no. The craving was just too strong. Mascara all over my face, I fisted the sheet and mustered up a tantrum that could put any two year old to shame. Sobbing, I shouted, "Matt, if you loved me you would get me a whopper!"

I knew I had done it now. Our marriage vows hung in the balance. He promised for better or worse and not having a Whopper in my hand was definitely the worst.

Matthew's mouth flew open, his mind preparing a response, and then – just as quickly as he opened it, he shut it, took off his glasses, turned off the light, turned over and went back to bed.

And I wept in the dark…for a loveless marriage…and a whopper-less life.

As the first rays of light began to peak through our bedroom curtain the very next morning, I awoke swollen-eyed and confused. Had it all been a dream? Did I really question his love for me because of lettuce, tomato, and a sesame seed bun? Sheepishly, I tiptoed from the bed and made breakfast. Maybe a peace offering and a few slices of humble pie would do the trick? I crafted the best apology I could and greeted him with it as he walked into the kitchen. Thankfully, I married a really good man who, not only forgave me immediately, but made plans to take me to Burger King that afternoon.

"I don't know what was wrong with me," I told my husband between bites. "I have never acted like that before."

A few days later, I found myself up again at midnight, but this time it had nothing to do with a cheeseburger and everything to do with the words that I kept hearing resonate within my heart as I tried to sleep: "Drive to Meijer." The words, as odd as they may have been, hit me like a semi-truck, or should I say a Burger King craving, and I knew that if I did not get out of bed, brave the wintery winds that awaited me beyond the door, and drive to Meijer, I may never sleep again. So, I went shivering and obedient and, this time, without waking my husband.

When I reached the inside of the store, I started walking to the pregnancy tests. As if pulled along by a force greater than myself, I practically ran into the shelf they sat upon. "Pick out one." Without a second thought, I grabbed the cheapest test I found, purchased it, and obeyed the voice within.

It was only when I got in the car the tears began to flow and the reality of what I had done hit me. Was this a cruel joke? I had laid this dream down. We were focused on the arrival of Abraham in a few months. Birthing a child was no longer on my radar. I had even stopped praying, laying down my dream at the feet of Jesus and trusting that He knew best…even if it hurt sometimes. This had to be because of what my mother had said at the family dinner and the weird burger craving. This couldn't be real. This couldn't be right.

Arriving home, I hid the box in the bathroom upstairs and fell back asleep beside my husband. Four hours later, I jolted from bed as if yanked by an invisible fist. "Go. Take the test." I again listened to the voice of the Lord and ran upstairs before my husband awoke. And there, on the bathroom floor, that small, secret hope became two, beautiful pink lines on a test. Tears of longing and fear became tears of joy and knowing.

God hadn't said, "No." He had simply said, "Trust."

Within days, we received the call that all of paperwork for our processing adoption had been approved and we should expect a call at any time informing us that Abraham was ready to brought home. It was then that it all made sense. God knew what we didn't. He saw the whole picture.

God hadn't said, "No." He had simply said, "Trust."

On the day that Abraham stepped off the plane and into my arms, I felt the baby move within me for the first time. Standing in the airport awaiting my son, my heart was overwhelmed – as it is often when I look back at the season of our lives – by the goodness of El Roi, the God who sees.

God hadn't said, "No." He had simply said, "Trust."

I prayed fervently over the next few months, that our baby would be a girl. After reading countless books on sibling rivalry between adopted and biological children, I believed that if we had a girl, it would be the best for Abraham – giving him time to adjust and embrace his new-found sonship. Looking back now, I often ask myself why I've so often felt the need to play "God" and shoulder the weight of planning our future – a future I cannot see.

I'm reminded of God's words in the book of Isaiah, "My thoughts are higher than your thoughts (Isaiah 55:8-9)." Like a pawn on a chessboard, we can only see what is before us and beside us. But God, from His higher perspective, sees the whole picture and how each piece fits together, moving each one strategically and thoughtfully throughout our lives. He sees what we can't. He knows what we cannot know.

So, when I said, "Girl," He said, "Trust."

Just six months after Abraham was placed within my arms, I found myself in a dimly lit hospital room pushing with all my might. My husband, so engrossed in the moment, let go of my legs. So there I was, holding up my own legs, pushing through contractions, crying and rejoicing—tired and energized all at the same time. Within moments, my baby boy, not girl, was born. Unable to breathe on his own, they rushed in medical staff, began oxygen, and I sat helpless, watching. My husband looked at me in desperation as I cried, "What is wrong with my baby? Why isn't he crying?" And then a warrior's bellow sang to my fears a song of God's reality. It was all okay. My baby was okay.

Jordan Mekai entered the world at seven pounds and eleven ounces. Holding him on my chest, singing lullabies to him and staring into those big, sea-blue eyes, I found myself drenching his soft cheeks with my tears of joy and thankfulness. He took my breath away.

I remember when Abraham walked into the hospital room the day after Jordan was born. I had worried how they would bond. I had agonized over what I had read in the adoption training books. I had prayed ceaselessly that God would unite them. And on that day, Abe entered the room with one mission: find baby brother. Touching his tiny arm with wonder in his eyes, he said, "My bruver. Mine."

From that moment, they were inseparable. Come to my home on any given day and you will find them up in a tree together, giggling and telling secrets. Abraham's deep, intellectual view of the world challenges Jordan's creative and vibrant imagination. In the same way, Jordan has taught Abraham, who often only sees situations in black and white, to paint with all the colors in God's universe. They are each other's yin and yang. No one could have created such a perfect match but God Himself. Watching them grow up and learn from one another is such a delight!

Where Abraham sees a car, Jordan sees an invention for time travel or an alien spaceship.

Where Jordan sees a perfect box to make a robotic head, Abraham sees a topic for discussion – "the power of recycling to save our natural resources."

When Abraham was paralyzed by social fears, it was Jordan who stood by him through thick and thin, always willing to stay with "Baba."

When Jordan felt discouraged by his small stature, it was Abraham who slowed down and let him win a few races, then told him all the things that his height made him perfect for…like fitting into the kitchen cupboards during hide-n-seek and curling into a ball to roll down the big hill at the park.

Every day I look at them together, God's plan makes more and more sense. God knew what we didn't. He saw the whole picture and He knew what was best. Romans 8:38 tells us that "He is working all things together for our good."

"He is working…" Even when it doesn't feel like it, even when you can't see Him - He's working.

"…all things…" Not just some, not just the good stuff, but ALL things.

"…for our good…" He always has our best interest in mind. He is for us.

Jordan Mekai Homan, born on September 7, 2006, is living, breathing proof of that.

Chapter 2...
Finding Joy

The day I found out I was pregnant for Shiloh, I felt equal parts delight and panic. Matthew had been struggling to find steady work for over a year. Most days, feeding the two children I already had required mommy giving my share to them to ensure they had enough. Our daily food groups centered around ramen, macaroni, and, if we were lucky, a hot dog. Because of the price of propane, we did without and made the best of a camper stove set upon our regular stove that was unable to be used. The house was cold. The kids were hungry. The parents were weary.

This was the life we lived. Hand-me-downs, canned goods from family members, and lots of praying for the money to cover each bill as it came in. Ever been there? I never thought we'd be...but we were. And it was scary. I had told myself before becoming a mother, that I would never let my children suffer or struggle or hurt.

I would fight for them, protect them, provide for their every need. And yet, here we were, struggling, suffering, hurting...and now, pregnant.

Calling my husband to tell him that I was holding a test with two pink lines terrified me. *What would he say? What would he feel?* He worked tirelessly to provide for us and had taken so many hits this past year. His shoulders sagged under the weight of responsibilities and burdens. He thought I couldn't see it. He tried to hide. But I knew. I saw. And I worried. *Could his shoulders carry one more brick?*

To my surprise, he took it like a champ. "Children are a gift, Niki. This is good."

Have I mentioned that I love that man? His smile began to ignite a small spark of joy within me, too, and before long, it had grown into a roaring fire. God had blessed us again! Surely, He would take care of us.

Following a Sunday service, just a few weeks after discovering that I was pregnant, my husband handed me twenty five dollars and said, "Niki, I'm so sorry, but this is all I have. Get what groceries you can." My mind flew to the long list in my purse and I immediately knew this would not be enough. There were diapers to buy, baby food to purchase, not to mention are son's special formula. Not wanting to make my husband feel worse than he already did, I kept these thoughts to myself and simply smiled. "Okay. I will get what I can. See you later."

Pulling into the grocery store parking lot, I pulled out my list and my cash. "Lord, you multiplied five loaves and two fish. You fed thousands from that small meal. I know that you can do it again. We need a miracle. I'm asking you to show me how to stretch this money to get the things we really need." Prayer complete.

I shut off the car, put the keys in my purse, and walked into the store. Grabbing the first available cart, I started down the bread aisle. We could survive without bread. I could roll the meat up with some cheese and the boys would love it. It would be okay. They might even think it's fun.

"Pick up the bread," a voice spoke from behind me, stopped me in my tracks.

"Pick up the bread, Niki." Turning, I saw no one.

"That was weird," I said aloud as I started moving again.

"Niki, pick up the bread. I will take care of you."

Picking up the bread, I threw it into the bottom of my cart, almost embarrassed by the foolishness. I knew I couldn't afford it. I knew I would have to put it back.

Yet, this happened again and again all through the store. I would hear a voice tell me to pick up the baby food, pick up the meat, pick up the pasta, and I would obey even though I hated myself for it. Face red from embarrassment, I approached the checkout. My cart was filled to the brim. There was no way this would all be just $25.

The beeping of the cash register mocked me. The bags filling with groceries laughed at my stupidity. Why would I listen to that voice? Why would I do such a thing? And then…

"Ma'am, your total comes to $24.99."

"E-e-excuse me? H-how much did you say?"

"$24.99."

Not waiting to find out if she was wrong, I quickly handed her my twenty five dollars and dashed away with my cart, yelling behind me that she could keep the change. As I put it all in my car, I read and reread the receipt. I couldn't believe it. Was this real? Had God just multiplied five loaves and two fish again?

In the months that followed, not only did God continue to provide for our every need, but He also provided my husband with a new job that gave us a steady source of income and our first taste of financial security.

On April 10th, 2008, Shiloh Alecia Ruth graced us with her presence. Born into a home that was battle-weary from a year and a half of struggling to make end's meet, it didn't take long after her birth for us to realize that yet again, God knew so much more than we did and His plans for us were so much better than our own. After a long, cold winter, she was our springtime.

Shiloh was a breath of fresh air to our family. She was a cool rain in a dry desert. She taught us all how to slow down and laugh again. She brought with her a rebirth of joy. With every toothless grin, every giggle, and every slobbery kiss, she reminded us of what we had forgotten – that God was faithful and a keeper of promises, that He had not failed and He would not fail us. God had known exactly what He was doing. We needed her. The world needed her. How could we—how could I—have questioned His wisdom?

Even now, if I close my eyes, I can see the three of them, Abraham, Jordan, and Shiloh, nestled in their toy room, surrounded by pillows and trains and big dreams. The three amigos: Jordan, the mastermind of every brilliant idea (ideas that usually began and ended with something they were not allowed to do…and duct tape. Always duct tape.); Abraham, the one who could figure out how to make all of Jordan's brilliant ideas become reality; and Shiloh, the smiling baby-sidekick who somehow got blamed for everything…even though she couldn't sit up without help. They kept me on my toes, teaching me new things all the time. Like how diaper rash ointment can also be used to gel your little brother's hair and toilet paper can also be used as a house decoration. Ah, those were the days. The days of "Three's Company"…but, alas, they would be short lived.

Only nine months after Shiloh's birth, I found myself staring at two pink lines again. Two pink lines announcing that our Isaiah Stephen was on his way. I approached this discovery with confidence, fully assured that if I could handle three – four would be a piece of cake. This wasn't my first rodeo. I had been pregnant before. In fact, I had become pretty good at it. How hard could another one be?

Fast forward six months. to a belly beginning to round out, a mother who was completely exhausted, and legs that decided not to work. Because Isaiah sat upon the nerves that ran along my lower back throughout his pregnancy, my legs often became numb and unusable. Refusing to call anyone to help me or admit my defeat, I crawled from one room to the other as the little ones followed, fixing lunch, changing diapers, reading stories, and making bottles until my legs would once again, regaining their feeling. I liked to call what I was doing "resilient" and "determined," but, what I should have called it was pride. And that pride was stealing from me the joy I had found in motherhood.

After the hardest pregnancy I ever experienced and a traumatic and failed attempt to deliver him naturally, Isaiah came into the world via c-section on September 18, 2009. He was eight pounds, eleven ounces of pure perfection. As the doctor worked with him, Isaiah began to fuss. I listened for my baby's first cry, but instead the sound that came from him was deep and rich and something straight out of the Incredible Hulk movie. The whole room silenced. Looking at me in bewilderment, the doctor laughed, "I've never heard a child sound like this before." I should have known in that very moment that this little boy, my Isaiah Stephen, had been born to break the mold.

As we left the hospital, I knew that now that the pregnancy was behind me, everything would be fine. I was "resilient." I was "determined." I was woman – hear me roar! But then I discovered that my sweet baby had a problem…he was nocturnal. When the rest of humanity slept, Isaiah felt the need to party. This led me to new levels of exhaustion I had never known existed.

Exhaustion that makes one take a shower with her clothes on and run into walls at two in the morning when she is rushing to make a bottle for the next feeding. Exhaustion that puts clothes away in the fridge and walks back to bedroom to change with the jug of milk still in hand. It was the kind of exhaustion that sits on your eyelids and refuses to allow them to lift…even in church. It was from this very tired, very empty well that I attempted to pastor, wife, and parent. The pride that I had labeled "resilience" and "determination" no longer felt like badges of courage to be worn and flaunted – they felt like burdens, reputations too hard to maintain. I felt ashamed. I felt embarrassed. I felt like a failure. Yet, I knew I needed help. I knew I needed to tell somebody. I needed to let somebody in.

Abraham had taught me faith. Jordan had taught me trust. Shiloh had taught me peace. And Isaiah? Isaiah was teaching me very quickly how desperately I needed God. **I couldn't do it on my own.** And this revelation brought me to another revelation that was equally important: **I didn't have to!**

James chapter one verse five says, "If any of you lack wisdom, let him ask of God, that gives generously and without preference and it shall be given him." Oh, how I clung to that verse and still do – every single day. This season of my life was one of brokenness – but not in the way we so often look at brokenness. I *needed* this breaking. Weariness led me to humility. Humility led me to my Savior.

"God, I can't do this on my own. I don't have what it takes to mother four children under five years old and pastor and love the people you've brought into our home in this season to love…and still be the wife my husband deserves. I'm so tired. God, it's too much for me. I don't know what to do. I need you."

It wasn't a pretty prayer. It was more desperation than poetry. It came with wadded up Kleenex, runny mascara, and spit-up-stained pajamas. My knees did not kneel at a grand altar. They knelt on a pile of dirty laundry. But there, I surrendered, in my laundry pile of Gethsemane. With one "Yes" I gave up my attempts to do it all on my own and in that "Yes," I found the JOY of motherhood again or maybe – for the first time. Real, true, genuine JOY that came from a life surrendered.

Chapter 3...
Facing My Greatest Fears

Psalm 34:18, "The **Lord is near to the brokenhearted** *and saves the crushed in spirit."*

Our fifth child, Gideon Drake, was to be our "final child," our swan song, our last dance, our finale…or so we thought. From the first moment we saw him, we were head over heels in love. When he was weighed, immediately following his birth, the scale read, "seven pounds, seven ounces" and my husband took it as a sign. If the number seven meant "completion" in the Bible, it must mean "completion" for our family as well. Oh, how wrong we were.

Not long after his birth, God began to draw our hearts toward adoption again…and again, we did what we do best: We made plans.

"We need another girl because Shiloh only has brothers."

"The child has to be less than five years old…and it can only be one."

How the Father must laugh with delight at our failed attempts to take His place! As the winter of 2012 rolled in, our paperwork was filed and we began to wait for the call – the call that would alert us that our daughter was on her way. And then life happened.

Journal Entries, December 2013 - January 2014

Day 1

Thursday, around 3pm, Gideon choked on a carrot piece and Daddy administered the Heimlich as EMT's rushed to the scene. After being transported to the local hospital, it was decided that a tube should be inserted and he be put on heavy sedation to help his lungs calm down and get the oxygen needed. They then transported us to a larger hospital where the doctors looked at x-rays and discovered his left lung had collapsed. They then sent us to the Children's Hospital for intensive care and a bronchoscopy. The bronchoscopy showed no more "choking hazards" but Aspiration pneumonia in the left lung (as a result of the choking incident). He is now still on the vent and under heavy sedation.

I sat there beside his bed, my sweaty three-day old clothing sticking to the pleather seat. Surely this wasn't real. Surely this swollen, lifeless body beside me wasn't my son. Surely all of this – the ambulance rides, the surgeries, the collapsing lungs, the blood clot between his brain and heart –must be a dream. And yet…I wasn't waking up.

Day 4

Last night, around 3am, Giddy Bear started to decline. After moving, suctioning, and percussions (as is routine every three hours) his oxygen levels began to drop like always, but this time, didn't want to come back up…I was asked to gather the family. We have not left his side. Right now he is receiving 100% of his oxygen from the vent. This can only last for so long before it is too much pressure for his lungs. I would usually try to sugar coat this, but I do want to let all those who love him be aware of where we are. We need God to move. There is nothing that He can't do.

The prayers I prayed over my son during those long days and nights often came out sounding more like undefinable groans than profound faith-filled prayers. They were raw and messy and real. They were imperfect and sometimes even angry. But it didn't matter. God met me there anyway. He met me in all my tear-stained brokenness and unresolved questions. He met me, not with judgment or disappointment, but with grace and immeasurable love.

I saw Him in the eyes of the compassionate doctor who squeezed my hand and promised not to give up, in the care of a nurse who gave me the wash rag and let me wash my son, sensing how desperately I needed to touch him. I saw him in the love of our family.

The way they rallied around us was a beautiful representation of what family was always meant to be. And I saw Him in the body of believers – all 2,000 of them – that joined us in prayer through his Care Page and Facebook updates. Our little boy brought together people from all over the world – his one life touching the lives of so many.

Day 30

Today. Today, we are going home.

As we stepped outside the hospital, the cold air assaulted my lungs. The sting of the winter chill felt good against my cheeks. It had been so long since I had been outside…so long since I had been home. The ride home was a quiet one. He looked out the window, I looked out the window. It all felt like a wonderful dream. Were we really here? Was he really coming home? Was this nightmare finally over?

Then the car stopped and the door opened.

"Moooooommmmmmyyyyyy!"

I had finally woken up.

Wrapped in my children's arms, the "Yes" heard was not my own, but the one of my   Loving Heavenly Father.

"Yes, Nicole. We're home. We're here. We made it. Rest now. All is well."

A little over a month after we returned home from Gideon's hospital stay, the phone rang. Matthew and I had been consumed trying to juggle our new "normal" – which consisted of weekly check-ups and multiple injections into our babies chubby thigh each day, swallow tests, and lung x-rays, carting brothers and sister along, in an attempt to squeeze in moments of togetherness. Our foster license was the furthest thing from our minds. In fact, I had completely forgotten that it had been approved. And then the phone rang.

The call came while we were sitting in a business meeting at our home. The older children were playing downstairs and Gideon, not yet ready to leave my side, was on the floor near me, playing with small toys. I had just begun to work again and felt as if, maybe – just maybe – we were getting the hang of this. Ignoring the call, I continued listening to the conversation around me. Then, that voice…the one that said, *'Pick up that bread,"* and, *"Drive to Meijer,"* spoke again to my heart. *"Pick it up. These are your kids."*

My heart stopped. My jaw dropped. Was this for real? Now, I had to answer.

"Hello, Nicole? This is (Case Worker's Name). We have these two boys – 10 and 6 years old. We can't place them in their county. Nobody wants them. I wasn't sure what to do, but then I thought about you two. Interested?"

Two boys?! This was NOT my plan, our plan – THE plan. What was God thinking?

"I will have to ask my husband really quick."

Running into the living room and waving frantically from the back of the meeting to get his attention, I pointed to the phone in my hand and tried to motion with whatever hand signals that I could think of that would mean "our case worker is on the phone and we have kids." Needless to say, he didn't catch my meaning. Puzzled, he excused himself from the group and followed me into the bedroom. I told him the news. I waited for his reaction. Surely, he would say no. This was not the plan.

"I hear a yes. We need to say yes. These are our boys."

Say what?

My heart couldn't agree more, but my mind was racing with questions and confusion. A voice shouted over the loud speaker in my brain: "This is not the plan. This is not the plan. This is NOT the PLAN!"

"Ok, Matt. I will go get them. You finish the meeting. Wait! What will we do with the beds? They are up in Shiloh's room! They have pink sheets!"

"No worries," Matt said calmly, "I will end the meeting, tear the beds down, move them to the boys room, and, well…they will just have to sleep with pink sheets tonight. We will work it all out tomorrow."

"Is this really happening?"

"This is really happening. Go get our boys."

Headlights neared and parked beside me, drawing me back into the present. My stomach filled with a thousand butterflies. I held my breath as I watched the door open to the worker's minivan and reveal our boys for the first time. Curly, unkempt hair. Long eyelashes. Big, brown eyes. From the very first moment I met Reuben and Peter, it was love at first sight. I wanted to memorize them, take a snapshot of their every detail. I never wanted to forget this moment – a moment when a mama's heart found the pieces that she didn't even know were missing. My entire being surged with joy and trembled with fear at the thought of it.

Everything in me wanted to run to them…and from them and the pain that loving them could cause. Those first few days, the hard reality of foster care, the unsurety of the future, the lack of a promised "forever" kept me guarded and unfeeling. I realized that although wrapped in packaging, the fear I felt in loving them was the same fear I felt in losing Gideon. I didn't know if I could survive the loss. So, I went through the motions of motherhood and smiled through my tasks, they were just that – tasks, motions, robotic responses that I knew a mother would give to a child – refusing to let my heart feel what it already felt – love. I wanted to love them. I did. But I didn't want to hurt. I wasn't sure my heart could take that depth of scarring. I had already endured so much in the past year. I just couldn't let myself hurt like that again, face that scary place of loss one more time. Until one day, when God met me, weeping over a pile of dirty dishes.

"Niki, you know the One who can heal your heart if it breaks. They don't."

It was God's fifteen word response to my prayer that changed everything. I knew what I had to do. Leaving the dishes in my sink, I went outdoors in search of my new sons. It was time to let myself love them, really love them unrestrained. **I knew that even if I lost them someday, I would never regret loving them.**

Those were the days of wonder, of learning to splash in mud puddles and dance in the rain. We spent hours outdoors introducing our new "city" boys to good ole country living. They milked a cow, hiked the woods, picked berries, swam in the lake, and went to bed each night with dirt between their toes. They were living a "childhood redeemed" and, if you have ever had the pleasure of watching one unfold, you will know that there is truly nothing like it. Amidst all the hard stuff – the screaming and crying and learning to trust – was the magic of rebirth, of new life, of second chances. It was breathtaking.

Just when I felt I had found the rhythm of raising seven children under ten years old, the phone rang again. Reuben and Peter had three younger siblings: one boy and two girls. Would we be willing to take them all? Without hesitation, we knew our answer was yes and Shiloh, our daughter, couldn't have been more thrilled. TWO sisters not just one?! This was her dream come true.

I prayed that her soft heart would not be broken through the process even as I prayed for my own. I had completely fallen in love with these five beautiful children. My heart longed for a secure forever, but my mind knew the truth – forever was not promised. Many nights were spent on my knees beside our bed, weeping. *"God, please give me the strength to let them go, if I must. But God…please don't make me let them go."*

Then the day came. Our case worker came to our home with the news that we could begin the adoption process. It was, as if, in that moment we all took a deep breath and exhaled for the first time in over a year. The room grew silent as we rested our hearts in the reality of her words. We would be together FOREVER. What an incredible gift!

"Um, Miss?" Reuben asked, as he pulled himself from the human pile they were calling a "group hug."

"I have a question."

"Yes? What is it?"

"Can we change our names now?"

When she told them that this was, in fact, an option, they all squealed with delight. It was as if it somehow solidified that we were indeed going to be a family forever. Peter knew right away what he wanted his name to be. Grinning ear to ear, tongue wagging through the gaps of his mouth where teeth should be, he declared, "I will be…Spider-Man Homan."

"What? You want your name to be…Spider-Man?' I asked in shock.

"Yup! Isn't that cool?"

I looked at my husband, my eyes sending him an S.O.S. message. This is not what I had in mind when we told them they could choose their new names. I was expecting James, or Jessie, or Howard – not Spider Man! Thinking fast, my husband replied, "You know…if we call you Spider-Man everyone will know your secret identity. But, if we name you Peter Parker (Spider-Man's real name) then it will be kept secret."

Peter Parker Homan. He liked the sound of that. And so did we. Not long after, Nevaeh Hope, Daniel Levi, and Hadassah Pauline had chosen their names as well. Nevaeh wanted a pretty name. Daniel wanted to be that "Lion-Tamer-Dude" from the Bible. Hadassah wanted to be royal. That left one – Reuben Nickolas Reno Homan. He spent weeks deciding what he would be called.

"How about John the Baptist?" he asked as we drove to my parent's home on a Sunday after church.

"John is a good name," I replied. "A strong name."

"No, Mom. Not John. John the Baptist. John the Baptist Homan. I want the whole thing."

"Ok. Well, I guess we said you could pick your name, so if that's what you want ---"

"No," he cut me off. "It's still not right."

Pulling out the list of names we had printed from the internet, he scanned the page whispering names to himself and shaking his head.

"No…no…no…YES! Mom, I got it!"

"Yea? What it is it?" I asked, quietly praying it was better than John the Baptist.

"Reuben. That's my name. My name is Reuben. What's it mean?"

Eyes blurring with tears, I pointed to the definition, "Son. It means first born son."

"That's me, Mom! I am a son! Reuben Homan, your son. I like the sound of that."

"Me too, buddy. Me too."

Chapter 4...
The Birthday Gift

October 24th, 2017 – my birthday. Matt and I drove silently in our empty car. So many thoughts were running through my brain. I had done this six times before and yet still, on this day, it felt like my first time. *Would they like us? Would we recognize them from their picture? How would we know if we were the right fit?*

At the very beginning of 2017, our children had begun to ask us to adopt again. They returned from Sunday School each week to inform us that when they listened for God's voice during prayer time, He told them that we were going to have more children and we needed to get ready. They started offering us their beds, their toys, and even their rooms for the new children. Every family meeting and dinner table discussion circled back to this topic.

"Mama, God is saying do this. You ready?"

At first, my husband and I laughed. They couldn't be serious! Or could they? Was this really God's plan? Could we even adopt more children? Would they even let us? Slowly, our resolve was softened by our children's persistence. They had planted a seed. God began to water it. Everywhere we went, He confirmed it. This wasn't just the ramblings of children. This was the call of God to our family. It was time. But…how?

It was hard to fathom finding an adoption agency that would look at us as more than just "collectors of children." Who would bet on us – two people in their early thirties, raising ten children already? Who would trust us with more – even one? Most people fear even letting us babysit their child, let alone keep it alive FOREVER. It all seemed so impossible. Yet, the call would not go away.

As I laid my head on my pillow each night, my heart whispered, "They are waiting for you. Go get them." As I folded laundry, tears flowed freely as I envisioned them running in from outside – wild eyed and joy-filled.

God, show us what to do, where to go, I prayed.

A few days later, He answered. My husband had called a local adoption agency on a whim. "So, maybe they say no, but, maybe – just maybe – they say yes. Niki, I've got to try. I will beg if I have to." No begging was required. They jumped at the chance to work with us, having just placed a child in a home where there were nine other children. They had no problem with the size of our family. In fact, they loved it. Before long, we were knee-deep in paperwork and home-study visits. Our children could not have been more thrilled.

When the news came that we could begin to look at the photos of adoptable children and place inquiries, the entire family crammed around the computer to look and decide. Day after day we searched. We only wanted one – maybe two. Age didn't matter. Needs didn't matter. One or two – that was our only requirement. Shiloh, the leader of the clan although not the oldest, who has often told us her spiritual gift is "dictatorship" – took the lead.

"Nope. That's not the one. Not that one either. Let's see. Hmm. Yup! There she is! That's the one."

Matthew and I sat stunned while the children around us eagerly agreed. This was the same little girl we had seen so many months before when we started looking. The same little girl who we had said "no" to because she had three other little siblings and we thought it sounded crazy for us to even THINK of adding four more children to our home. Of all the children on the registry, THIS is who they point to?!

Clearing my throat, I asked, "You do know that this little girl isn't alone, right? She has three other siblings that come with her. This one –"

"Awww! I LIKE THAT ONE! YES!"

"…And this one – "

"She will be my best sister friend!"

"And this one too."

"He is ADORABLE. I want him. Let's ask if we can adopt them."

My heart swelled and tears formed in the corners of my eyes. Was this real life? Was this really happening? Was God going to allow us the privilege of raising these four beautiful children as our own? Looking at my husband, I asked, "Well, should we just…ask?"

He smiled and nodded. The children cheered and went off to play. Closing the computer, I thought to myself, "If only we listened to God as well as our children."

"Niki?" my husband asked, breaking into my thoughts. "How are we going to fit in the van?"

"I'll get you a Moped," I answered only half joking.

"God will provide. He always does. Let's just see what happens."

Fast forward again to my birthday – October 24th, 2017. Here we were – in the car, about to turn into the parking lot where we would wait for our first face-to-face meeting with our four new children. The case workers had said yes when we had called about the possibility of adopting. YES! The papers had been signed. The home had been thoroughly studied. This was it. The final piece of the journey – meeting and building relationship with our new sons and daughters.

Parking the car, Matt looked at me and smiled. He has always been the cool and collected one and I've always been more of the "super-excited- passionate-fired-up-sugar-with-a-whole-lot-of-spice" girl. He is the mac to my cheese. Looking at him, I knew that no matter what happened inside the building, I would forever be thankful for this man beside me who consistently reminded me, "Babe, God told us to live a yes…let's just do that and trust Him." Resting in his peace (since I didn't have a lot of my own), I jumped out of the car and entered the building by his side.

After waiting, for what felt like all of eternity, the door finally opened and in walked four of the most beautiful children I had ever seen. Under their arms they carried the scrapbooks we had made for them. I could see the recognition on their faces and the insecurity in their eyes. They knew us. We were the two grinning adults in the photos. Wary and shy, they followed their foster mother down the hallway as we followed. They looked back from time to time to see if we were still there.

The room they placed us in was lined with chairs. There was a little table in the corner and a shelf with a few toys against the outer wall. After making introductions – the case workers, foster mother, and lawyer sat down I the chairs and watched as we stared at our new children and they stared back at us.

Nothing, absolutely nothing, can prepare you for these moments. What do you say? Who do you reach out to first? What brings down their protective armor? What proves to the case workers and foster mother that this—that we—are the right choice?

"Nice to meet you," the words came from my lips sounding much more confident than I actually felt. "I like your scrapbook."

"You made it," Brionna, the oldest, spoke up, obviously having been nominated to be their spokesperson.

"Yes, we did," I said directing the conversation to her, "It has our children and our dogs inside. It shows you our house too. Do you like the pictures?"

Nodding, she opens it up to the first page.

"That's you."

"Yes, that is me and Matt," I say, pointing from him to the picture.

"Who is this?" she asks after turning the page.

"That is Gideon. He is our youngest right now."

"He looks like a friend."

"I am sure He would love to be your friend."

"Okay." Turning a few more pages in the book, she stopped and asked, "And this picture?"

"That's the girl's room."

"Is that my bed?"

"Yes, it will be."

"I put my picture in this book too. Wanna see?"

Moving her hand quickly over the pages, she reached the very back of the book, and held it up.

"I'm in here now too."

"I like that. It's a really good picture," I said, unsure of what she wanted me to say.

After looking at me for a moment to make sure I meant what I said, she closed the book and shrugged. Turning to the others, she gestured for them to come closer.

"It's okay. We can color now."

Looking at my husband, he smiled. I guess we had passed the test. Matt took a seat at the table and picked up a crayon. "Can I color with you?"

Before long, both Phoebe and Brionna were talking his ear off while they drew flowers and rainbows with Crayola crayons.

This left me with boys. I sat on the floor and began setting out the things we had brought with us to play with. Among them was a package of matchbox cars. Thank you, Jesus, for matchbox cars! Within minutes of opening the box, I had become a mechanic and they had become world-renowned racing legends. Before we knew it, it was time to leave.

Somewhere in there, the oldest, Brionna, had discovered it was my birthday. She made me a play dough cake and sang to me. We looked at her scrapbook again and she asked more questions about our home. Before we left, they all asked when we would see each other again and Brionna made sure I took the picture she drew to her new friend, Gideon.

After the visit, we walked to the car trying to find the words to articulate to one another what we felt. But all that would come were tears.

"Yes. These are our kids."

"They are even more beautiful than their pictures."

"How did we get so blessed?"

A few weeks later, all the children met for the first time – the fulfillment of the promise God had spoken so many months before, the fruit of my children's refusal to give up or be silent about what God has shared with them. A month after that visit, we started overnight visits and in March of 2018, our beautiful Brionna Ariel, fearless Phoebe Joy, gentle Ezekiel Keefer, and adorable Jedidiah Jeremiah came home.

Driving home with them and all of their belongings – knowing this would be the last time we would have to make this trip, I was overwhelmed by the goodness of God.

"Mama, you is mine forever now?"

"Yes, baby. Forever."

If you had told us sixteen years ago that this would be our life, we would have laughed in your face. Never in a million years could we have written this story. Each of our children represents a "yes" that we said to God, not fully knowing what that "yes" would mean – the lessons it would teach us, the gifts it would bring us, the tears we would shed because of it, and the immeasurable joy that would be found on the other side of it. The word "Yes" has forever changed our lives and we will never regret one "yes" we said to Him.

This is our family.

This is our Yes.

And saying, "Yes," was only the beginning.

Chapter 5...
Yes to Our Normal

The alarm clock chimes, but we are already awake. First, our daughter needed to use the restroom, then our son wanted to come in and chat about the dream he had – the one in which he is a ninja and has a trained pancake as a sidekick. The story draws a crowd and, before you know it, our room is filling with tiny humans.

"Why do we even set an alarm?" I ask my husband as we roll out of bed and the children exit our room to awake the sleeping stragglers.

Before long, our house is full of laughter, conversation, debates, negotiations, and the craziest wardrobe ensembles you have ever seen. My sons believe that you can never have enough patterns in one outfit. The more, the merrier. They are known for rotating the same pair of plaid shorts for weeks attempting to match them with every striped shirt they own. They like to complete the look with two mismatched socks and a button-up shirt…of yet another plaid design. We had hoped that having the older boys help them pick out their clothing in the morning would help. Turned out, they are also firm believers in stripes and plaids as a clothing combination.

After they are dressed, chores begin and so does breakfast preparations. It seems this – my time spent in the kitchen – interests people the most. I am often asked, "How much food does your family consume in a week?" or "What is your weekly grocery bill?" Another common question is, "How do you feed them all?" And the answer to that one is simple. You just…do it. You learn what they like and what they don't like. You buy on clearance. You make a list and stick to it. To me, a breakfast of thirty scrambled eggs, a gallon and a half of milk, and entire box of pancake mix, and the complete contents of a large jar of syrup is – well – "normal." And because it's normal to me, it doesn't feel like a burden to make. It just feels like a Monday. A Monday in which 250 dishes will be washed, five to six loads of laundry will be done, 32 snacks will prepared, 51 servings of food will be cooked, and my children will say my name 999,999,999,999 times. I often liken them to the seagulls I so often see swarming forgotten donuts in the grocery store parking lot. Except…I am that donut.

This brings me to my daily breakfast of champions: burnt coffee. It starts beautifully. My husband makes it in my "Mommy" cup. He knows just the right amount of sugar and cream. It's the stuff dreams are made of. But then…

"Mom, she is wearing my shirt."

"Mom, we were just hugging and, I don't know how it happened, but he got punched in the face by my fist."

"Mom, does this match?"

"Mom, can I wear your headband?"

"Mom, when do we get a snack?"

"Mom, Peter is hot-wiring the lamp again."

Before I know it, my coffee is cold and I'm reheating it only to realize, it's time to start school. So, pushing the start button on the microwave, I walk away to call my crew into the dining room to get started. I love this time of day. I love watching their eyes light up when they see something they have never seen before. I love the way they smile and sit a little taller when they master a skill that they had felt impossible. I love their questions, their love for learning, but, I won't lie, some days, it can feel overwhelming. On these days – the overwhelming ones – I have been known to put myself in time out so that I can regroup and keep going. Time Out is awesome. And it's even better with a cup of coffee. So I grab it out of the microwave only to discover…it's cold. again. Starting the microwave back up, I head to time out. Take a deep breath. Pray. And dive back into the crazy beautiful that is my life.

When I finally come up for air, it's lunch time and that cup of coffee I reheated again is – you guessed it! – a cold, burnt shell of what was. At this point, I surrender and guzzle the soot "formerly known as coffee" and start making lunch. Playtime follows along with errands, activities, dinner, and baths – our lives are not much different from yours.

When finally night comes, we gather together to read. Once the couches are filled, children begin to find space on the floor – curling up under soft blankets, doodling in notebooks, holding stuffed animals close. A few gather around the table to put together a puzzle – our latest obsession and, without fail, a few find their way to mama's lap. I love this part of the day. The smell of their freshly-washed hair, the warmth of their bodies curling into mine, the sound of their gentle breathing—they feel safe with me. What a wonderful feeling. No matter how difficult our day has been, no matter what we have had to walk through that day, no matter how many times they have screamed at me or pushed me away in anger, in these moments, we come back to each other.

Right now, we are reading the biographies of missionaries we admire: D.L. Moody, Amy Carmichael, Mother Theresa. My husband and I often lose ourselves in the stories. We have to wipe our eyes from time to time, stopping to regain our composure. These stories, these lives, have a way of putting things into perspective, a way of reminding us that it's worth it and that we must, no matter what, keep going. By the time we finish the chapter, the room is quiet and all are at rest.

"Yes!" we think to ourselves. *"This will be easy!"*

And then…it happens.

We say, "Bedtime."

Oh, the cacophony of sound that one word can birth into a quiet room!

"No. Five more minutes, please?"

"Mom, can I sleep in Jed's bed and he sleep in mine?"

"Mom, I think I have a disease. It's infectious and you need to check it. I should probably sleep with you."

"Mom, I'd like to talk about the end times and dissect the book of Revelations with you right now while you try to put a herd of wild children to bed."

It's complete and utter chaos. I wish I could paint a different picture for you, but…imagine a zoo where all the animals were placed in the same cage. And then multiply that crazy by a million. That's bedtime.

Next comes what I like to call the "holy hush." There are really no adequate words to describe the joy I feel as the house quiets and my toes slide in between the sheets and comforter, finding their way to the perfect place in my bed to take off my socks and leave them for my husband to find.

Ah, it's the simple things. This is a joy that can't be packaged or purchased - it's one that creeps in slowly like a tide and washes over the very depths of my soul. Oh, how I love to annoy him. I have decided this may be my love language——the sixth one that no one talks about. It's what motivates me to put my cold feet on him while we watch a movie and never put the toilet paper on correctly—although I do try. It's what pulls me from the bed each morning to leave all the lights on, drawers open, and fold the towels wrong. Actually, it's done without my knowledge. Who knew there was a proper way to fold a towel? And yet, I thoroughly adore his voice, calling me from the laundry room,

"Niki…which kid folded these?"

And I thoroughly enjoy responding, "Not a kid. Me."

Because somewhere, between the awkward pause and the lesson on proper folding, we will laugh. And not just a soft chuckle. We are talking full blown, belly laugh. If there is one thing we Homans are good at, it's laughing—even when we shouldn't be, even when our car is on fire, even when the dishwasher is shooting bubbles all over the kitchen, even when laughter is probably not appropriate. Thankfully, my husband decided years ago that if we had to choose between laugh or cry, we would choose to laugh and that is one thing we Homans have figured out how to do well.

Oral hygiene, however, is not. Case in point: The Community Toothbrush. My boys live by one simple rule: "**What's mine is mine and what's yours…is mine.**" And before I can continue, this story, there is one important thing you need to understand. Someday, my E! News Hollywood Story will begin and end with this – "Throughout her life, Nicole was known for having what can only be called as a "sheer hatred and disgust" for anything tooth-care related."

I HATE the smell of toothpaste. I HATE to touch someone's toothbrush, clean toothpaste off the sink, and don't get me started on SHARING my toothbrush. I don't just hate toothbrushes and toothpaste, I genuinely CANNOT be near them. (Now, before you worry that I've made it to age 31 without ever using a toothbrush, let me be clear: I BRUSH MY TEETH. But I don't want anyone else's tooth-care items near mine. Girls got some strict boundaries on that. I even purchase the children new toothbrushes every month to ensure everyone has what they need…and don't need to come within 500 feet of mine. I have a drawer FULL of spares. And yes, I'm aware I have issues. Jesus is still working on me.

So you can imagine how I feel about (insert Jaws Music Theme) the "Community Toothbrush." And here is where our story begins…again.

My boys share a bathroom. It is the kind of bathroom you would expect from ten boys. A public urinal. An indoor porta john. A "smell and wear" pile of dirty—yet not yet "dirty enough" to go to the laundry—clothing options. I do my best to train them well. They do chores daily. They help during the weekly "cleaning day." But it's ten boys against one bathroom. We're fighting a losing battle.

Within this bathroom, there are drawers. PLENTY of drawers to hold important items – like deodorant and TOOTHBRUSHES and toothpaste and….TOOTHBRUSHES. And every week, when I go to the store, I ask: "Boys, what do you need for your bathroom? Do you have… (and I go through a very specific and detailed list ensuring they have what is needed…and "bet your bottom dollar" (sang with an Annie voice) that I make sure tooth-care items are on that list.

A few days ago, as the boys slowly made their way up the stairs after morning chores (which is a mixture of WWF, Mixed Martial Arts, and organized "piling"), I asked the group, "Did y'all brush your teeth?"

"Yes, Mom."

"Of course."

"Sure."

Looking at Gideon, one of my youngest, I ask pointedly, "Did YOU brush your teeth?"

"Yes, of course. I used my finger."

Heart palpitation. "Your…finger? Why not a, I don't know,…TOOTHBRUSH?"

Shrugging nonchalantly, he picked up his breakfast plate from the counter and responded, "Because I don't have one."

Eye twitch. "When did this happen? I just went to the store. You guys didn't say you need any toothbrushes."

Through a mouthful of breakfast, Gideon says innocently, "It's okay. I've been using Reuben's."

"Say…whaaaaaat?"

"Yea…lots of us have."

"What? Wh-wh…why don't you tell me that when I go to the store every week and ask if you need anything?"

"Because we don't. We can just use his."

Oh, sweet heavenly Father. A community toothbrush in the public urinal. Things felt like they were headed downhill real fast. When I asked for a show of hands as to who had been using the "community toothbrush," multiple boys raised their hands. I could barely stomach the news. Toothbrushes were top on my list for the grocery store that day and spares were handed out immediately.

Oh the joys of mothering boys.

People often ask me for snapshot of my life. They ask what my parenting style is. But this…this "community toothbrush" and smelly bathroom reality….this IS a very REAL look into our ordinary.

Raising kids is MESSY and sometimes it's downright HARD. Sometimes you have life-marking, memory-making moments together…and sometimes you just get through it.

Like scrubbing toilets, I've never heard of a mom who loves to scrub toilets…but we do it…because we know it's all part of this messy, beautiful adventure we said, "Yes" to.

My "snapshot" is no different than yours. And my parenting style?

It's a three-step process:

1. Get On Your Knees.
2. Throw Up Your Hands.
3. Shout, "Dear God…What do I do?"

No joke. 99.9999% of parenting steps *way* beyond the line of what I can do on my own. I need His wisdom. I need His strength. I need His help. I NEED Jesus. And, I've come to discover that that's okay. It's OKAY to not be able to do it on your own. It's OKAY to need a Savior. He knew we needed Him. That's why He came.

I have a pretty good feeling that this won't be my last "community toothbrush." I also have a pretty good feeling that before they all graduate and move on, I will be keeping the Oral-B company afloat with all my tooth-care purchases. But…there has to be a silver lining in this somewhere, right? At least my boys have learned to…share?

Chapter 6...
Yes to Intrusions

     In my bathroom, there is NO solitude. If Mommy is putting on make-up, she is a captive audience for the last song you wrote, a discussion about magnetism and electricity, or a twenty minute adaptation of "The Sound of Music". This is the prime time to share what you have been dying to share with her. The other 23 hours and 45 minutes of the day have just been preparation for THIS moment.

     "Mama? You see my finner? You see my hand? Mama? Mama? Why you not talking? Look, Mama. You see my finner?"

     "Can I eat this?"

"Mom, can you sew this button on for me? Here, I'll hand it in."

"Mom, so there's this girl…"

It's amazing that I ever get out of those oversized sweatpants and brush my teeth. They have so much to share and so many "finners" for me to see. When people ask me, "How many children do you have?" I now answer, "I have "When did I take a shower last?" many kids." Seriously. I can't remember when I shower anymore. I can't remember if I shampooed my hair. I can't remember if I shaved. I can't remember because the closed shower curtain has become my children's "Confessional" and, like a catholic priest, I'm busy offering forgiveness and a listening ear. Something about knowing I'm there but not being able to see me creates a desire in all of them to step into a place of extreme honesty and that honesty usually needs my attention more than my armpits do.

"Okay, so it looks pretty good, but I wanted you to know, I may have cut bangs with the school scissors."

"You did – what?"

"First, let me say, I love the outfit you picked out…and then I need to tell you…"

"Where is she? Tell her I'm on my way." I respond, hurrying to wash at least part of my armpit first.

"Mom, I found this empty snack bag under my pillow and I'm pretty sure I maybe ate it all."

"You maybe ate it?" I clarify, knowing full well it's been devoured.

"Well, like my stomach hurts and I may puke from all the chocolate, so…like…maybe I probably did."

Oh, you, closed shower curtain. You mystical, magical thing that stirs in the hearts of my young the ability to share their deepest secrets while I loofa. I would know nothing—nothing— without your super powers.

A few years ago, as I returned to the bathroom, realizing I had only shaved one armpit and needed to remedy that, I discovered a large brown streak down my white shower curtain. It's height and positioning left nothing to the imagination. It wouldn't take a rocket scientist to conclude that this wasn't any ole stain. This was P-O-O-P of the human variety. I knew exactly who to call.

Sauntering in, he took one look at the stain on the curtain and shrugged. He didn't even try to deny it. After all, we were in the "Confessional."

"Look, I ran out of toilet paper. What's a guy supposed to do?"

There are moments in parenting that the answer seems so obvious to the question being asked, I find myself dumbfounded by their inability to figure it out on their own. This was one of those times.

"Um…I don't know…maybe you could ASK FOR SOME?"

His eyes wide and astonished, he replied, "Wow. That's a great idea. I'll do that next time."

Needless to say, the white shower curtain is no longer with us. May it rest in peace. Yet, no matter the color the curtain, the confessions keep coming…and I keep listening, because, at the end of the day, that's all they want in the first place—somebody who listens.

That's really all I want too. Some days, motherhood is hard. Some days, I feel like giving up. Some days, I wonder if I'm fighting a losing battle, if I have what it takes, if I can wake up and do it all over again. On those days, I often find myself, fists to countertop, tears filling the sink while the shower's hot water washes down my drain. Sometimes, that's why I don't shower, because I took all of my time…confessing.

"God, help me."

"God, I got upset again…raised my voice…I hate when I do that…help me."

"Please, forgive me."

Oh how I love that He meets me there, never shying away from my mess, never hiding from my mascara-stained face, always gracious and good and true.

He meets me. He gives me strength. He lifts my head. He forgives all my short-comings. He wraps me in His grace. And then He calls me to do the same for them, my children, with all of their confessions, some small, some big. Can I give what I have received? Can I share what I have found? I always thought I could, until one day not long ago.

Kneeling down in front of my daughter, I brushed a hair out of her eyes hoping to see her more clearly. Her two, angry almond-shaped eyes pointed to the floor. Her wild hair stuck carelessly to her sweaty forehead, her fists clenched ever so tightly. Everything about her dared me to come close…and yet begged me not to. Growls and sobs mingled together from her tiny lips and my heart felt cold at the sound of it.

Her words stung today. Like salt in a wound, like pressure on a bruise, she spoke to place in my heart already broken by words I had heard a million times before. I'm not a good mom, they hate me, and they wish I was dead. She was not the first, nor would be the last to tell me these things. I had been down this road more times than I could count and it always started and ended in the same exact place.

First, they would scream and then they would hit me. Some spit, some kicked, some threw punches, but all used me as the target until finally, they would melt into tears and ask for forgiveness. I could walk this road in my sleep.

"Please forgive me, Mommy! I'm so sorry!"

How many times had I heard that?

How many times had she pledged her undying love for me and promised she would never hit me again only to do it again the very next day?

Everything in me wanted to give her what she deserved. Grounding, loss of privileges, early bedtime, the joy of cleaning the house…consequences started dancing across my mind. Which would I choose? And that Voice again…HIS voice.

"Hug her."

"Excuse me, God. Come again? You want me to do what?"

"Hug her."

Surely, He did not expect me to do that. After all she had done? After the way she had treated me? This had started long before sunrise and now, as the sun was going down, I just wanted to be DONE.

"Hug her."

I looked into her eyes that still challenged me. Could I do this?

Taking a deep breath, I opened my arms. Lip quivering, countenance changing, she threw herself into my embrace. As her whole body relaxed, I watched her guard slowly come down—if not for forever, at least for the night. She looked so peaceful in my arms, so content. The light from the hallway peeked through the door and unto her soft cheeks as I looked at her one last time before placing her in bed. The sight was enough to take my breath away. She was, she is…priceless.

"All day long," Father God said, "I stretch out my arms to a rebellious and contrary people." Oh, how I have been there. Rebellious? Check. Contrary? Check. Check. And I haven't just been there…I've been THAT.

He could have treated me as my sin deserved. He could have thrown in the towel, called it off, turned away. No one would have blamed Him, questioned Him, or doubted the "rightness" of His actions. He had EVERY RIGHT to be done and yet, here I am, daily running headfirst into the undeserved grace of Daddy God.

This image brought me to tears as I left her room. Because, you see, I needed GRACE just as much as she did. How many times could this verse have been applied to me?

"All day long, I stretch out my arms to my disobedient daughter,
Niki, who keeps running in the wrong direction!"

Oh, what manner of love is this?

We live in a culture that says, "Scratch my back and I'll scratch yours." "Get even." "Pay them back!" "If you want my respect, earn it!" As the world around us screams for "retaliation" and "paying for one's mistakes," Jesus calls us to love like Him and loving like Him will look a lot like saying "Yes" again and again to…GRACE.

Even if that grace is given during a shower curtain confessional at the Homan's house.

<u>I Love You. Period.</u>

I love you.

I love you even...

I love you even when you break my favorite china plates.

I love you even when you leave the hose on all night and flood the basement.

I love you even when you write on my freshly painted walls.

I love you even when you scream that you hate me.

*I **LOVE** you.*

I love you when...

I love you when you break the toy I bought you.

I love you when you let the dogs off the chain.

I love you when you steal from my purse.

I love you when you sneak into the kitchen at night to eat the food I planned for the next day.

*I love **YOU.***

I love you no matter...

I love you no matter how many times I have to drag you out of a store kicking and screaming.

I love you no matter how many times you embarrass me in public.

I love you no matter how many times you lie to my face.

I love you no matter how many times you break my heart.

I love you.

I love that dimple that dents your caramel cheek as you smile.

I love the way you giggle.

I love the sound of your voice singing the worship song from Sunday as you do your chores.

I love the tiny freckles that emerge with the sunshine of summer.

I love the kindness that hides inside your heart...it's there. I see it. Amidst all the mistakes, there IS beauty!

I love that you call me mom. Of the millions of women in the world, I'm the one who gets that privilege. It makes me proud, makes me walk a little straighter, and causes me to hold my head a little higher. Even on the bad days...I wouldn't trade you for all the money in the world.

You are MINE.

And I love you. Period.

Chapter 7...
Yes to the Unexpected

    I always start vacations with such expectation. I build them up in my mind. What might be a *"short trip up north"* becomes an opportunity for a glorious, life-altering, EPIC adventure in which we will all get along wonderfully...and hold hands as we skip down the beach...with the waves of the Great Lakes tickling our toes...and angelic harps serenading us...as we take the most perfect family photo ever...in matching blue polo shirts...and everyone will be smiling...and...Are you getting the picture?

    I want Disney World Magic AND a Hallmark Holiday Special rolled into one perfect family vacation, but then...the car blows up on the side of the highway in heat of mid-summer or a child gets the flu and pukes all over your vacation dreams or you hit a traffic jam that pulls from you the ability to make a child-safe porta potty out of a sand bucket and a prayer and I realize my dream is never going to be my reality. I have fourteen kids. Fourteen. So, now, I have two choices.

1. I can fall into a puddle of my tears and eat my body weight in melted chocolate (that was hidden in the suitcase just in case I found myself in said moment).
Or…

2. I can keep moving. Because beyond this moment is another moment, and it might be beautiful, the stuff dreams are made of…and I refuse to miss it.

One of our last Florida vacations was not what I expected. It had many challenges. On one of the hardest days, a day I was fighting with everything within me not to just pack it all up and head home early, we decided to take the kids to the beach to see the sunset. Swallowing my salty tears, I pasted on a smile and loaded them in the van.

As we drove by palm tree after palm tree, I told myself that tonight was the night things would change. I would have fun and I would make them have fun, too. We would make our memories before we left for home. And, come hell or high water, I would get my vacation photo.

Climbing out of the van, I gathered the family on the beach. The water was breathtaking. The sand tickled our feet. The wind tossed our hair this way and that. We breathed in the ocean air and experienced the lightheartedness of the atmosphere. I could almost taste the "perfect vacation moment!" I knew this was it!

"Okay, kids. Take your shoes off and put your feet in. Mom is gonna take a picture."

Scene set, I grabbed my phone and prepared to snap the pictures I had waited all vacation to take—the ones where we look happy and like we actually like each other. Funny how my children took my instructions to put their feet in as permission to dive head first into the waves. Before I could stop them, I was photographing the sagging drawers and wrinkly shirts of kids who had fully immersed themselves in the ocean.

And that's when I had to make the choice. What would I do?

Would I fall apart or would I fall in?

I chose to fall in.

Kicking off my sandals, I ran towards the water knowing there would be no turning back. When my boys saw Mama was okay with getting wet, it wouldn't take them long to seize their moment. Sure enough, they met me at the shore line – laughing, splashing, and pulling me deeper. I could feel the love of God crashing into my heart like the waves of the Atlantic Ocean. As we played and I knew I would never forget this moment together. I knew that years from now, THIS would be the story I would tell of this family vacation. The story of when everything went wrong and yet, somehow, was completely right.

The reality is this: over time the "mess" of family vacation fades away and what we are left with is a great story of sticky ice-cream fingers splashing salty waters and the delightful sounds of giggles and ocean waves. How do I know? Because, when my brothers and I gather together over the holidays, the stories we tell are of the vacation when our car decided it would only drive in reverse or the one when mom turned all of our clothes pink. We tell these classic family fun fiascos with belly-aching and eye-watering laughter. We LOVE these stories. We CHERISH them. Not because everything went perfectly, but **because, when it all fell apart, we didn't**. And that makes for the best stories.

As a child, I had a vision in my mind of what true love looked like, and just like my fairy-tale vacations dreams, it came straight out of Disney. I can still picture it in my mind: Cinderella's breathtaking ball gown gently swaying to the rhythm of the music as she was held securely in the arms of her Prince. Without one hair out of place, without one misstep, they gracefully moved across the dance floor as if they were meant for THIS moment. Lost in each other's eyes, they found themselves out on the balcony of the castle before they knew it. Gone was the crowd. Gone was the ballroom. Only the song remained,

"So this is love. So this is what makes life divine..."

Oh, Disney...You had me at Prince.

As a child, I bought this love story hook, line, and sinker. I WOULD find a Prince. We WOULD fall in love in five minutes. We WOULD live in a castle of perfection basking in our perfect love and have the most perfect life EVER. THIS was love.

Oh, Disney...How wrong you were.

Fast forward to thirty-three-year-old me, cleaning up my daughter's puke in the middle of the night. And what do I hear? Father God singing over me:

"So this is love...So this is what makes life divine..."

Oh, what a laugh we had together—my Father and I.

He followed the serenade with a movie reel in my mind that proved better than any Disney Love Story. It included images of my husband holding me while I cried on the floor of the hospital; midnight feedings of babies who hated sleep; loads and loads of dishes; and endless laundry piles. In this film, love was portrayed as messy, hard, exhausting, unselfish, relentless, and faithful. It was so much more than a moment under starlight. It was a lifetime in the trenches.

A few years ago, the flu hit our home in full force. One after the other, the children dropped like flies. My days were spent moving from room to room emptying puke buckets, checking temperatures, administering medicines, and sanitizing everything. At the same time, we battled the plague, our dogs decided to bring home fleas. You heard me – FLEAS. Imagine it. A family of our size battling both the relentless flu and the demon flea epidemic all at once. It was, to sugar-coat it and not make it too terrifying, a complete and total nightmare.

We tried everything to get rid of the fleas. EVERYTHING. Nothing made a difference. It was as if they had built up immunity to every single spray, bomb, and powder on the market. I can't put into words the level of exhaustion my husband and I felt after two weeks of this. "God," I cried, "Please do something. We need to sleep. We need breakthrough."

Then, just like that, the miraculous happened. Everyone started feeling better. The color came back into their cheeks. The fleas finally died. Hope started to spring up.

"Babe," I whispered afraid to say it too loud and jinx it. "We might actually get to sleep tonight...like uninterrupted sleep!"

That night as we laid our heads down on our pillows, we breathed in deeply, savoring the peace. It felt glorious to sink our bodies into our soft mattress and wrap up in our clean, newly-washed, free-of-puke down quilt. This was the life.

Fast forward a few hours. 3 A.M. to be exact.

"MOM! Peter is puking!"

Jumping from our bed, we ran through the house. Peter slept on the top bunk. So, if Peter was puking, where was that puke going? What we found in the boys bedroom was nothing short of a crime scene. Puke everywhere. And seeing puke, made them all puke. Kids were gagging everywhere you looked. Beds were covered and the room was drenched with the stench of sickness.

"Okay, someone fill up the cleaning bucket and bring us rags. We've got to clean this up."

Always the administrator and organizer of our chaos, my husband took charge and started cleaning. He worked on one triple bunk while I took the other. The boys all stood watching on the other side of the room cradling their pots, pans, and mixing bowls just in case.

Working at ferocious speed, Matthew reached the bottom bunk and crawled in to wipe it down—not knowing that puke had splattered on the back of the beds against the wall. As we worked in the silence, too exhausted to say anymore, I heard an awful sound.

Plop.

The sound could only mean one thing. Turning to look at Matthew, I saw what I feared. Dripping from the wall onto his bald head was a big, pile of puke.

"Don't say anything," he calmly said as he closed his eyes tightly.

"Don't say a word."

That's when it hit me—the uncontrollable giggles of total exhaustion. My shoulders shook, my sides hurt, my eyes watered. I couldn't hold it in. Thankfully, neither could my husband. There we sat next to the triple bunks, rags in hand, puke everywhere, laughing so hard we couldn't speak.

Y'all, sometimes life is hard.

Sometimes…it downright stinks.

That night all of the tears I had held in, streamed down my face as I snorted and howled at the insanity of it all. This was definitely not the fairy tale I had imagined as a young child of what love would look like and yet…this WAS love – real love.

When everything was falling apart, we weren't.

We were in this together, one puke bucket a time. Even in the mess of sickness, delirious with exhaustion, love could be seen and experienced and felt. A love that stays, that endures, was all around us and in us for one another. It's wasn't glamorous, but it was glorious and permanent.

For the rest of their lives, our boys will have this memory of their parents at their worst and love at its best.

Yes, to this kind of love story and these kinds of vacations–even when it brings me flus and fleas and exploding engines and cars that only drive in reverse. God never said it'd be easy, but He did say it'd be worth it. And, man, do we have some good stories to tell from it.

Chapter 8...
Yes to Not Giving Up

"It's been nine days since I took a shower."

The realization of my personal-hygiene fail hit me like a stray baseball to the face. When had I ever let it get this bad before? Assessing the damage in the mirror, I finally admitted the truth I had been ignoring.

"Dry shampoo can no longer fix this."

It was time for an intervention. And by intervention…I mean hot water and a gallon of soap.

Opening my closet, I searched for something other than yoga pants to wear. With over half the children sick, the past few days had been a blur and it was time to do something to reclaim myself, but more importantly, to reclaim the fresh scent that use to accompany me everywhere I went. I missed that. My husband did too.

I'd love to say that this was the only time my personal hygiene has sacrificed itself on the altar of a motherhood, but Maury Povich would determine that to be a lie.

I have found myself, sometimes daily, asking questions like, "Niki, did you brush your teeth today?" I have thrown myself into the shower on early Sunday mornings only to notice I was fully clothed when I started to soap my sweatshirt.

Shaving my legs is no longer a right, it is a yearly privilege. Sitting down beside my husband to watch a movie a few months ago, he pulled my legs up into his lap. Placing his hand across my legs, I quickly informed him, "You may not want to do that. I can't remember the last time I've had time to shave."

A-ways patient and easy going, he responded kindly, "I'm sure it's fine, babe."

And then...

"Oh, wow. You weren't joking."

No. No, I wasn't. Although, I wish I had been.

Some of the reason for my recent lack of hygiene has to do with arrival of the teenage years in the Homan Household. When you have two six-year-olds, who think, "Oh, how cute. It's like they're twins." When those six-year-olds become two smelly teenagers…things look, and smell, a little different.

As I write this book, we have, under the roof our ever-shrinking home, seven children that are pre-teen or full-teen. It is rare to find a bathroom that is not being used by one of them to style their hair yet again or style someone else's hair or change their outfit for youth group for the 3,456th time.

"Bathroom Time" has become a cherished and rare commodity. My lack of it has made me consider the wisdom in one of my boys' latest inventions: The Suspended Porta Potty.

I came upon this invention not too long ago, as I walked through our woods. Looking up into the canopy of one of our large oak trees, I found two sets of dirty little boy feet dangling from the branches. Stopping near the tree, close enough to hear, yet far enough to not be noticed, I listened to their hilarious conversations. I will never understand the workings of little boys' minds. The things they value:

1. A blue sock with fried eggs all over it (seriously, they all fight over it, and I don't even know if it ever had a match).

2. The amount of worms they think they could swallow before puking.

3. How they could destroy a mountain lion with the use of only a toothpick and a rubber band (a total "MacGyver- move").

4. The length of time they could go without taking a bath (I almost interrupted here to let them know I had them beat).

5. Where to find the perfect trees to climb.

Smiling at their wildness and innocence, I made my presence known with, "Hey, boys, how is it going up there?"

And that's when I saw it. Hanging from an old, frayed rope piece next to my boys was MY red cleaning bucket.

"Boy, what is MY red bucket doing in the tree?"

"Being useful."

"Useful for WHAT?"

"It's our bathroom. This way, we don't ever have to come down."

Silence as I process this information

"Have you used it already?"

"Yup!"

More silence as I process

"So, you are telling me that there is a bucket of PEE hanging from my tree?"

"Yea, but don't worry. We dump it when it's full."

It was then, folks, that I can honestly say I wasn't sure what to feel. Was it total disgust that I had a bucket of my boy's pee looming over my head? Or was it total gratitude that they hadn't decided to dump it while I was under it? Or could it possibly be total respect for their ingenuity and commitment to stick it out in that tree whatever the cost? I mean, my boys invented a suspended porta potty! I can just see them trying to market their product.

"Yea…so you take a thread-bare rope and you let your little brother who still can't fully tie his shoes tie the rope around the branch so you don't ever have to come down from your favorite tree."

Our family will be millionaires.

Staring at the red bucket, I shook my head and said the only word that came to mind as I looked at that monstrosity. "Wow."

Yup. That's all I said. "Wow." And I walked away.

I needed time to collect my thoughts. Because, as crazy as this all was at the time (which, in all honesty, isn't feeling so crazy now that we have so many teenagers and bathrooms are hard to come by), I felt like, somewhere in all of this, there was lesson. No, not in my boys' choice of bathroom (Although, like I said, the more I think about it, the more I think it might not be such a bad idea), but quite possibly in their willingness to do WHATEVER IT TOOK to stick it out and to STAY in that tree, no matter what.

We have a saying, "No back door." It's made us hold on through the heartbreaking moments of life, the ugly disagreements, the complete and utter exhaustion parenting can bring, and the occasional hairy armpit. No matter what we feel, no matter how broken we are, no matter how bad it gets, for us, there is "No back door."

Years ago, one of my children decided to test this theory.

He broke my Grandmother's china. He threatened me with his fists. He told me I was a horrible mother and he would never love me back. Hours, days, weeks were spent loving the unlovely. And it was hard.

Please, don't nominate for sainthood as you read this. Know that my reactions to these words and actions, were much like what your own might be. At the end of the day, I threw myself on the bed and wept. My husband reached for me, pulled me up to his chest, wrapped his arms around me and reminded me, "It's worth it, Niki. Don't give up."

So I got up the next day and I kept loving—day after day after day. Until the day of our family garage sale. That is the day everything changed. It started with a really bad haircut. And when I say bad, I mean…horrific.

This son of mine had decided to sneak away while we had customers at our sale. Going into my husband's bathroom drawers, he pulled out the razor we used for haircuts and decided he needed one. As the hair fell into the sink, he realized what he had done. It looked awful! Picture a chia pet and a spotted jaguar's baby.

Now, it's funny. Then, it was devastating to him.

What would the kids think at school? Why did he do this? He couldn't cover it up. He couldn't make it better. He had to come out and we would see it. Surely, he thought, this would be the thing that would make us give him back.

Pulling his hood as tightly as he could around his patchy, bald head, he came back out to the yard where our garage sale was taking place. Looking up from the money box, I knew right away something had happened.

"Bud, what's up?"

No response.

"Bud, take off your hood."

No response.

"Bud, I asked you to take off your hood."

Slowly, his hands went to his head and pulled back. The children around us gasped and giggled. This made him angry. Lashing out, he told us again how horrible we were and how he couldn't wait to get rid of us.

"That's too bad," my husband calmly said, "because you're never getting rid of us. We love you even right now with this really bad haircut."

That night, as my husband repaired the damage done to his hair, the house was silent. He was silent. No angry words. No rage. The next day, I found a note from him:

"Mam, I leov u."

Friend, there is so much to be MISSED by giving up and walking away, yet there is so much to be GAINED by digging in our heels, sticking it out, and saying "Yes" to whatever it takes.

I have determined within my heart that even if it means my personal hygiene suffers at times and I have to climb a tree to use my boys' invention because all the bathrooms are full of children – I'm not giving up. I'm in this for the long haul – no back door.

Suspended porta-potty, here I come.

Chapter 9...
Yes to Redefining Everything

It was a showdown at the Homan Corral. Everyone was silent. You could have heard a pin drop as her two brown eyes glared at me, unflinching. Her fists clenched at her side, her feet firmly placed on the ground, a pack of wild elephants couldn't have moved her from her spot.

"What did you just say?" I asked in disbelief, sure that I hadn't heard what I thought I heard. Sure that my child would never talk that way. And then…

"You heard me, B&$%#," she spat out with the fluency of a studied linguist. My ears couldn't handle the reality of what I had just heard. My sweet six-year-old knew curse words – like, a lot of curse words…and she used them, aiming them at me with all the marksmanship of Robin Hood in an archery tournament. Picking my jaw up off the floor, I exclaimed, "Excuse me? What in the world?"

"You heard me," she began again.

"I heard you," I quickly interjected, cutting her off before more profanity could roll from her tongue. "And now hear me. Go to your room."

I needed a minute to process what had just happened. I couldn't believe it. My little baby girl just…she knew words I didn't even know! Hanging my head in disbelief, I plopped on the couch and sighed. "My kids would never talk that way."

Then it hit me. My reality check. She is my kid and she talks that way. It doesn't make me a bad mom. It doesn't make her a bad kid. It just – is. It's our reality and I have to be okay with that.

In this pastor's house, our six year old sometimes swears. Is it getting better? Yes. Does it still slip in moments of anger? You bet. And guess what? She is still loved. She is still amazing. She is still our kid. Our kid who occasionally says the B word, but also always has a hug and a handwritten card to make you feel special. She's imperfect, yes,….but she's also wonderful. I am blessed to be her mom.

Years ago, at the very beginning of my motherhood journey, my husband challenged me to let go of the incredibly high expectations I was placing on him and our son, Abraham. He used words like "suffocating" and "boxing him in." His words shook me. Spoken tenderly, but honestly, they hit me exactly where they needed to. I realized that I had set the bar too high – for myself and for everyone around me.

My prayer became a simple one: "God, redefine family to me." I knew there had to be more. I knew I was missing it. The word "redefine" in the Webster's Dictionary means to, "define again, reformulate, reexamine, and reevaluate especially with a view to change."

Somewhere along the way I had picked up unrealistic standards for family. I not only expected perfection, I demanded it. My tone had become harsh. My words were unfiltered and littered with disappointment. They weren't measuring up. I wasn't measuring up. We were all miserable.

It was time for change. I knew it started here—with God reformulating and rewriting my definition of family. What He taught me, astounded me. It was so simple, so easy, so…freeing.

Home is a place for learning, not perfection." This lesson changed my life. I parented differently, pastored differently, loved differently after embracing this simple truth. It began with God revealing to me, in so many big and small ways, the depths hidden within his command to "love one another (1 John 4:7)."

On any given Sunday, I watched a prostitute and a third grade teacher, an ex-convict and police officer, a drug addict and a theologian share a pew, share a hug, share a prayer. They held hands and sought the Lord together and in this, this loving of one another—in all of their differences and brokenness—they discovered something so beautiful, so holy. They discovered a family.

It was imperfect. It was messy. There were disagreements. There were hurt feelings. Yet, there was also forgiveness and mercy, the ability to love the unlovely and embrace the imperfect in the perfect love of God. I watched the body of Christ be the body of Christ, and, for the first time in my life, began to see what I had missed all along—this had never been about perfection. This was about growth, about God taking us from "glory to glory." He cared more about "growing" somewhere than "going" somewhere. He loved the journey, walked it with us, taught us along the way. He used "iron" to "sharpen iron." Some of our greatest lessons being taught in relationship with one another. He met us in the mess. He made us more like Him.

I realized that home needed to be safe place for this to happen. It had to be a place where mistakes were draped in forgiveness and covered in love. It had to be a place where there were second chances, thirds, and even fourths—a place for learning, growing, trying again, not just for my kids, but also for me. It was okay that I wasn't the perfect mom. It was okay that I wasn't raising the perfect kids.

Do I want my daughter to swear? No. Does she? Sometimes. Is she learning that there are other ways to express herself? You bet. And while she learns, she will be loved. Not when she learns, WHILE she learns. See the difference? True, genuine God-love cannot be earned. It is not reserved for the deserving, the over-achiever, or the perfect child. He loves us now, right this very moment, whether we are climbing ladders of success or crawling out of the deep pits of our failed attempts. He loves us period. And, because He loves us, He doesn't leave us there. He calls us to higher places. This is grace—not the license to sin, but the power to change.

Some of the most powerful, life-changing moments we have had in this home have been built around a genuine "I'm sorry." It's been in our weakness, as Paul the Apostle once wrote, that God has shown Himself strong. Often the ugliest of days have ended the most beautiful. I can't explain it. I don't know how He does it. He just does, as we say "yes," breathe deeply of His love, and pray this simple prayer, "Lord, make us more like you."

He is redeemer. The one who "buys back, repurchases" and "wins back" what has been lost.

Maybe it's because of my years working with children from two parent homes; children being raised by single mothers and fathers; children being born to teenagers who were still children themselves; children in the system; children who had been abused, neglected, told they were a mistake.

Maybe it's because of my visits to orphanages throughout the years—seeing babies lying on mats craving the safe, comforting touch of another human; watching children play in the courtyard with a deflated basketball for hours.

Or maybe it's because of my years as a foster mom and now, as the adoptive mother of eleven—teaching my children how to play; showing them how the car wheels move when you push it back and forth; where to put their feet on a bike; how to pretend.

Maybe it's one of these, or all of these, that have become my reason WHY. Why I'm so incredibly aware of the GIFT that childhood is and so GRATEFUL for a God who redeems.

On the day of our last camping trip, last summer, we decided to roast marshmallows over a fire on the beach of lake Michigan. It was sunset and the sky was breathtaking. Shades of pink and orange danced across the crystal blue water. Gathering on the beach, we listened to the waves crash against the shore and as my children watched the sky, I watched them getting closer and closer to those tempting waves. I'm not sure who "fell in" accidentally first, but within five minutes, they were jumping the waves - jeans, t-shirts, sweatshirts, and all - and giggling at the top of their lungs.

The scene moved me. So much so, that I had to grab my camera and take a picture...or two...or twenty. Different than my last attempt at a beach vacation photo shoot, this time I remained dry— well, maybe not my eyes. I didn't want to forget this moment. I wanted to soak it down deep into my soul.

Pushing the record button, I snuck closer—the sand beneath my bare feet was sacred ground. I didn't want my children to stop. I wanted a recording of these carefree giggles. These were the giggles of a childhood REDEEMED and they deserved to be remembered.

Adoption has opened my eyes to things I didn't want to see. I've come face to face with the effects of abuse, starvation, and drugs—not in a newspaper headline of a city I've never been to, impacting people I will never meet, but right here in front of me—in my city, in my children. It has been eye-opening, heart-wrenching, and life-changing, but adoption has also opened my eyes to things I NEEDED to see, things I had taken for granted. Like a clean bed to sleep in, hot water for a bath, three meals a day, and the privilege of playing outside. Not only has God redefined family for me, He has redefined everything.

Adoption woke me up, and I'm not just referring to forfeiting sleep. I met children who cowered at any sound that resembled a gun shot. I taught a teenager how to brush his teeth for the first time. I sat with them and showed them how to play—how Legos work, how play dough is used to create. Everything was new. Everything was miraculous to them. Things I had taken for granted, I now found myself so grateful for. Their childhood isn't the only thing that has been redeemed. My wonder has too.

"Mama, look at this. A bug on the bottom of that leaf. You see it? All the colors. I touch it? Yea? Ok. Now you. Look, Mama, so beautiful."

Looking at the world around me through my children's eyes, I see so much that I was missing. My walks through the woods have slowed. They make me look under each leaf, discover the beauty hidden under a rock, close my eyes and listen to the moving current of the river. They have taught me all the things a stick can be. From Moses' staff splitting the great Chippewa River that runs through our hometown to a sword to battle dragons. According to my children, no two sticks are created equal. Each one is to be picked up, examined, and celebrated.

"Look, Ma! I got the perfect one for carving! Ooooh, wait. This one is even better! Can you believe it?"

Slowing the pace has not always been easy for me. It has pushed against my natural inclination to keep up the pace. Yet, in slowing down, I have discovered it was not only the beauty of God's creation that I wasn't seeing—it was people.

My children have taught me what a gift it is to have people in your life. God has used them to redefine for me what truly has value in this life. They cherish every get-together, fellowship time, potluck, and Christmas party. Noses smash against windows as they watch for the cars to pull up into the driveway and shouts fill the house as they see the ones they have been so impatiently waiting for.

I have been told so many times, "Oh, these kids are so blessed to have you and your husband," but what you must understand is this, WE are the blessed ones.

On one Christmas morning, while the other children happily tore open their presents, squealing for joy at each discovery, one of my daughters sat, uncomfortable, staring at the box with her name on it.

"Do you want to open it?" I asked gently. She nodded.

"Okay," I encouraged, "Go ahead. Just like the others."

Standing up, she walked toward the box and placed her hand timidly on the top. Softly rubbing her hand back and forth on the paper, she asked, "Mom, how? How I do it?" Her voice was a little louder than a whisper and I strained my ears to hear her amidst the noises in the room.

"How I do it?"

"Do what?"

"Open it."

That's when it hit me. She wasn't opening her presents because she didn't know how to. I was determined to change that. Wrapping my arms around her, I brought her hand down to the folded side of the wrapping paper.

"Grab a hold right here," I said enthusiastically.

"Now pull back and…hurray! You did it. Let's do it again."

Piece by slow piece the wrapping paper began to fall away to reveal the new kitchen set that lied beneath it. Oh, how she loved that kitchen and oh, how I loved watching her awaken to parts of childhood she had yet to discover, parts of belonging she had never experienced, parts of family she had been missing.

THIS is why it is worth it. The sleepless nights, the exhaustion felt deep into the marrow of the bones, the chaos, the overwhelming to-do list, the never-ending home repairs – all of it – made worth it in one of these terrifically ordinary moments. I look out my window and listen to their giggles and watch their bikes race up and down the driveway and whisper to my soul, "They are safe today. They are loved today. They are KIDS today." This is our redemptive story. This is family redefined.

Chapter 10...
Yes to Waiting

I say, "I love you." I say it again and again. And yet, he doesn't understand. His fragile heart argues, "But they said they loved me and now they're gone!"

I say, "You are mine." I say it again and again. And yet, he can't grasp it. His mind, consumed in fear, screams, "But they said I was theirs and they hurt me, left me, and told me I was the problem. How long until you do the same?"

I say, "You are worth fighting for." I say it again and again. And yet, he doesn't believe me. All of the pain and anger and confusion and fear comes to the surface, a living, breathing, active volcano of rage. He needs a target. He picks me. Doors slam. Screams echo through the house. Insults are spit from his mouth. It can be easy to wonder...will he EVER understand? Will he ever grasp it? Will he ever believe it?

I have come to the conclusion that adopting a child is much like plowing a field, over and over and over again. Most of the days are spent repeating the exact same words and actions - proving yourself faithful, trustworthy, unlike those of the past. It's monotonous at times. Rejected on a daily basis. And yet, you plow.

I plow because I know he's in there—hiding, under layers of protective armor; guarding what is too scary to reveal. I know nestled in his growing body is still my sweet little boy cowering under cloaks of insecurity and when he finally lets go, he will need me. He always does. As the shaking fists and cruel insults dissolve into tear-stains and broken-hearted sobs, he always cries, "Mama, don't leave me. Don't ever leave me." The sobs of a young man "too old" to cower on a bathroom floor and beg for his Mama…who sits right outside the door.

"Mama, I'm so sorry. I don't mean to do it."

I plow because of those moments—the ones that follow the pain. The ones where a strong young man is scooped up into the arms of a Mama as he rests in forgiveness and second chances.

"I don't deserve to be loved," he groans.

Rock-a-bye, baby.

"I don't deserve you, Mama," he weeps.

Hush now, don't cry.

"I love you, Mama," he whispers as his wet cheek presses against my own.

You are my sunshine.

I plow for those moments when silence falls, sleep invades, anger softens to grace. Sweet healing takes place and for one incredible moment, he receives my love. And that one moment gives me hope for millions of others...and they are coming. I know they are.

Because seeds grow.

Because Harvest Time does come.

This land I've plowed, these seeds I've planted, these years I've sown – they matter. HE matters. And I refuse to give up and miss the harvest that's coming.

One of my life verses has been James 5:7 and 8:

"Therefore be patient, brethren, until the coming of the Lord. See how the farmer waits for the precious fruit of the earth, waiting patiently for it until it receives the early and latter rain. You also be patient. Establish your hearts, for the coming of the Lord is at hand."

I have to believe that. I have to hold fast to this truth – seeds grow, harvest comes. If I don't, then what am I doing? All of this loving, this teaching, this discipling, this MOTHERING – is not a waste of time.

Years ago, I read an article in a magazine written by a mother of an autistic child. She encouraged families to celebrate the wins, no matter how small. I often find myself so focused on the distance between where we are and where we want to be, that I forget the distance between where we are and where we used to be. I count the losses instead of the wins. I forget how far we've come, and in forgetting, I tend to allow discouragement and hopelessness to burrow its way into my heart and my resolve to keep moving forward. If I give into the frustration, to the anxiety of "not meeting the expectation," I get so caught up in how much farther we have to go, that I stop moving altogether. Today was a great example of this.

I have a son who came to our home unable to tell me any of his letters or write his name. He could count to ten, but had no idea what the numbers looked like. The paperwork and professionals told me he had what is called a "global developmental delay" and had the IQ of a 4-year-old, with no signs of ever improving.

Guess what?

Today, that boy read a book to me, answered 3rd grade history questions, wrote his numbers to 30 without help, did addition regrouping, and wrote a sentence I could understand.

You'd think I would have done a happy dance. Instead, **I felt discouragement try to wrap its grimy fingers around my hope.**

"Wow, he still is pretty behind."

Immediately following this thought, came another one…

"BUT LOOK HOW FAR HE HAS COME!"

I almost allowed the distance between where he is and where (I think) he should be STOP me from celebrating the distance between where he is and where he used to be. I almost lost a moment to praise my son and rejoice in his win!

God has done a good work. God is AT work in my son's life. There is harvest. The seeds are growing.

As a mom, I can't forget that. For my children. For others around me. For myself, God is at work. He is doing a GOOD work. I can't allow discouragement, anxiety, or hopelessness to steal joy or cripple me from moving forward. I can't let it ruin my day. You can't either.

Not long ago, I was staring into the biggest, brown eyes I had ever seen and questioning if I'd made the right choice. He was fifty-five pounds of wild energy. The loudest voice ever placed within a pint-size package. When he first arrived, I feared I may never get to know him. Each day, every day, was sun up to sun down screaming. Most days, he spent in bed. He shook when I touched him. He ran when I called him close. He took everything I said the worst way possible—twisting my words, misinterpreting my heart. He lashed out in anger. My mama's heart was ripped to shreds. Nothing I did made him happy. No matter what I tried, I just couldn't break in to his heart.

"Did I make a mistake?" I whispered to God through my tears night after night.

"Am I not what he needs?"

"Is this how it will always be?"

After one year of his non-stop screaming, I reached a critical point—the moment where you can choose to give up or get up and keep fighting.

Hiding deep within me was the cry of my deepest fear, "This might be hopeless." After months and months of doing everything I knew to do, he still couldn't make eye contact. Every touch of my hand to his skin, to lotion, bathe, or get him dressed, resulted in jerks and shakes. He still refused to sit on my lap. I had to ask him to hug me good night. Affection was uncomfortable. I didn't want to say it out loud, but I feared this would be how it always was and I feared most that I didn't have what it within me to endure.

Grabbing a dish towel, I went to work on the kitchen attempting to take my mind off the sound of his screams. As I worked, one of my oldest, came in to the kitchen to find me. Wrapping me up in his perfectly-warm bear hugs, he sighed, "Well, look how I turned out, Mom. He'll be okay." Insert a weary mother's hysterical sobs.

Memories began to flood my mind of moments with him years ago, when I wondered if we could endure another month, another week, another day.

"I can't give up. Harvest comes."

I determined in my heart then and there to embrace the journey, no matter where it led and no matter how long it took.

This is the part of the story where I wish I could say, "And that was that. The next day, he woke up and everything changed." But that wasn't our reality. Sometimes God answers our prayers immediately with a crack of thunder, and a lightning strike of the miraculous. And sometimes His response comes more gently—dawning slowly like a sunrise on a summer morning. Bit by bit, we see God at work. We witness His faithfulness. With every gradual, glimmering sunbeam that pushes back the dark curtain of night, we watch a miracle unfold before our eyes. That's how it was with my son. One day at a time. One small victory after another. Then one day, he reached up and held my hand everywhere we went. He jumped in my arms and cuddled me for a long while as we talked of dinosaurs and pizza toppings.

We smiled at each other.

He looked me in the eyes.

The shaking stopped.

The screaming subsided.

The fear melted away.

I heard his giggle—a great eye-watering, hold-your-belly, squeal-like-a-piglet giggle that will delight the hardest of hearts.

I met my son, piece by little piece, and I loved him—deeper than I ever thought possible.

When I look at him now, I see why our "yes" was worth it, why it mattered. How could we have ever survived without his endless supply of really bad knock-knock jokes that make us laugh the very moment we need it most? What would life have been like without his goofy dances, his wise insights, his thoughtful love notes, and wild energy? We could have missed all of this. We almost did. If not for a hug and a reminder from our older son that if we don't give up, harvest comes.

Chapter 11...
Yes to the Lessons

"Niki, he's gone and we can't find him."

Tears burned the back of my eyes and overflowed down my cheeks. Grabbing my keys, I rushed from the church office and threw myself into the car. My hands shaking, my heart pounding, I put the keys into the ignition and white knuckled the steering wheel as I prayed,

"God, show me where he would run."

Turning out onto the road, I began to drive towards town. The silence in my car was deafening. The space felt hollow and empty. I fought hard against the fear that tried to seep its way into the very depths of my weary soul. He would be okay. He had to be okay.

After what felt like an eternity, my phone rang and I hurried to answer it. It was my husband, his voice strained with worry. Someone had spotted him. We finally had a location and it was only a few blocks away. Fueled by hope, I quickly turned my car around and began scanning the sidewalks.

"Please, God, help me find him and help me get him in this car."

That's when I spotted him—a black coat and dark hat in the midst of a crowded street. I pulled up and rolled down my window.

"Come on, bud, get in. We were really worried about you."

"No."

Cars began honking behind me. I was holding up traffic. I didn't care. All I could see was my son. My son who needed to come home. My son who I loved with every fiber of my being.

"Get in or I will call the police."

I knew this statement would shock him and gain his attention. He looked up to see the line of cars behind me and rolled his eyes.

"You need to move. You are in the way."

"I'm not going anywhere until I have you," I insisted.

His shoulders slumped and he breathed a heavy sigh, "Fine."

Slamming the door, he got in and buckled up beside me. He wouldn't look me in the eye. He made no attempt to reconcile. We just drove away in silence. In that moment the wall between us felt too tall and thick to scale. The emotions of the day formed a large knot in my throat, making it feel impossible to swallow. I dialed my husband.

"I have him. He is okay."

It's all that I needed to say. It's all that I could say. Relief washed over my soul like the soapy waters of a warm bathtub. I had him. He was okay.

We drove in silence. He stared out the window, arms wrapped tightly around his chest. I kept my eyes on the road commanding myself silently not to cry. What words were there to say? What could I say that I hadn't already said? What would make a difference? I waited for some brilliant quote to fall from heaven, but it never came. So, I said what I always said, "I love you forever and no matter what. I love you just as much today as I did yesterday. Nothing changes that I love you," and then I opened my door and went inside.

I would love to say that was the last time he ran away, but it wasn't. I would love to say that things immediately changed after that, but they didn't.

And this was my undoing—a good undoing, the kind that HAS to happen.

I tell him now that God used him to make me a better parent because as our relationship unraveled, things within myself were exposed that I needed to see. Things like fear. Fear of this world and fear of losing my children to it. Fear of living life without them. Fear of what might come. Things like anxiety. Anxiety that came from the pressure I put on myself to be the best mom and raise the best kids—as if this in some way validated my very existence on this planet. I needed him to be okay, because if he wasn't, I fully believed it was my fault. If I had loved more, been more patient, used a kinder tone, played more Legos—then maybe he would have been better, maybe he wouldn't have run away again.

Anxiety and fear are a toxic combination. They swallow your sleep. They consume every waking thought. They devour your free time.

Simply being near my son led to tension migraines and heart palpitations. I couldn't screw this up. I didn't want to lose him. He needed to be okay. I saw everything he did as a rejection of me, his every action screaming into the very depths of my soul, "YOU FAILED! YOU FAILED! YOU FAILED!" and, finally, I couldn't take anymore.

After a day of non-stop tears, I put on my walking shoes and headed out the door. I needed a break. I needed a breakthrough. As I slowly stumbled down our dirt road, I mindlessly looked out over the vast farm fields, while whispering desperate prayers to God, for help. Along the way, I saw a dandelion. It stood out bold and yellow against the freshly plowed field, immediately reminding me of a picture my son, Ezekiel, had painted the day before.

After listening to an audio version of *The Secret Garden,* I'd asked the younger children to paint a picture of their dream garden and share it with the class. Many filled their paintings with apple blossoms, water lilies, and bright, red rose bushes. Not Ezekiel, though. There, in the middle of his green, green, very green paper (he really likes that color), was a simple, yellow dandelion. Not two or three. Not a patch of dandelions. Not a garden of dandelions. Just one, solitary dandelion.

"This is the flower I would have in my garden," he proudly told his brothers and sisters. What most would call a common weed, was, to my son, the best of all the flowers.

Caught up in this memory, I continued to stare at the dandelion as I approached where it was planted along the dirt road. Slowing my already turtle-like place, I bent down and picked it up, planning to bring it back to my son, a memento of his "dream garden." But as I did, I heard the Father's voice, so softly yet so clearly say to my heart, "Niki, the way you see things is not the way I see things. The way you see this situation, is not the way I see this situation. Where you see a weed, Niki, I see a flower."

For the rest of the night and on into the morning, these words, spoken by a loving Father, consumed my every thought. I needed to know: How did He see things? And how could I begin to see them like He does?

In the days that followed, God began to show me things that I had been blinded to. I realized how much of my life had been spent trying to validate myself through achievement. What I had described as a "hard work ethic" was actually "a need to be valuable." I took on motherhood, as I took on life—as one long, drawn-out interview for a place of eternal value. The competition was cut-throat, incessantly trying to prove my worth. If all my children turned out well, people would see I had what it takes and my Father would see that I was a valued member of this team. I had somehow missed that I had already been accepted and approved, quickly reading over the pages of the training manual that told me that I had value on the days that I crush this thing called motherhood…and I also had the same value on the days I didn't. Somewhere along the way, I had forgotten that **God wasn't looking to me for results. All He wanted was obedience.** And in all of my striving to prove myself, I had forgot how to just BE myself.

This truth set me free. Not only could I love my children at a deeper and truer level, I could also love myself. This was one of the many life-changing lessons I have learned along my journey of motherhood—lessons I am so thankful for.

As a young mom, I assumed that I was the teacher and they were the students, when, in truth, we all are just students learning as we go. Some of the lessons are easy, even fun to learn. Others are hard and painful. But as we embrace the lessons, we grow, and as we grow, we bloom.

One of my children's favorite places in the world is the Stimson's farm. It's full of vibrant colors, delicious smells, good food, and deep love. From the tiny kittens curled up on the porch, ready to play, to the fruits, vegetables, and flowers growing everywhere you look – this is a child's dream. Mine, too.

I strap on my bucket and head out to the raspberry patch with such delight. I fully enjoy the time I spend with my children there in that garden, soaking in sunshine, chatting about nothing and everything, and picking berries for jam.

Jordan has a great picking method. "One for the bucket – plop! One for me – munch!" Of all of my children, he gathers the LEAST take-home berries and returns home WITHOUT FAIL as the messiest. But, oh, that berry-stained smile!

This past week, as we lost ourselves in the raspberries, my daughter, Nevaeh, poked her finger multiple times on the thorns. Her "Ouch!" would carry over the breeze to my ear, over and over again.

"Mama," she said in a tizzy, "Why God put all these berries in these thorns?!"

Just as quick as it came, her frustration left when she spotted a friendly kitten exploring near our patch, but I was left pondering her question. It reminded me of a conversation just a few days before with my Daddy (always the wise one). He had shared with me that often in our lives the greatest lessons are "carved out in pain."

The fruit of Humility is usually carved into us by "being humbled."

The fruit of Selflessness usually comes with much "dying to self."

The fruit of Meekness? That often comes with the destruction of our pride.

And for Nevaeh, the fruit of raspberries came with some thorns.

The reality is this: "Let this attitude be in you that was in Christ Jesus" doesn't happen overnight....it's going to take some carving, some chipping away at our rough edges, some deeply planted truths, some hard lessons, not just for our children, but for us, too.

I remember the day, that Jesus began to awake me every morning with these words, "Feed my sheep." As soon as He would speak them, I would reply, "Yes, God. Show me how to feed Your sheep." Day after day, we would do this, and day after day, my honest reply became a burning passion in my heart. "God, show me how! I

WANT to feed your sheep! I want to LOVE like you! Yes, God! Give me sheep to feed."

So He did.

He gave me sheep to feed. Not actual sheep (that might have been easier), but people, real, live people that needed to be fed. My response? Whining. Complaining. Belly-Aching. I down-right got angry and started yelling at God.

"But, I don't want to. But, it will cost me this and that and this and that....and what about this, God? Did you forget about this? I can't give this up!"

His voice cut through my frustrations with the softness of a mother's touch and the clarity of a judge's gavel, "Remember when I told you to feed my sheep?"

"Oh." I whispered under my breath. *"THIS is what You were talking about."*

What followed this brutally honest conversation with my Daddy God were some hard lessons on living UNSELFISHLY. I had to come face to face with the ugliness of my selfishness.
I had to lay things down I didn't want to lay down. It was painful. It was messy. **Yet, in the thorns, He grew FRUIT.**

It is rarely a fun process and I may even shout, "Ouch!" a few times along the way, but when I walk away with a basket full of fruit and taste the sweetness of a life lived with Jesus, IT IS WORTH IT.

My kids aren't the only ones being changed by Jesus. I am too. Loving them has required me to take long looks in the mirror and stare into the face of my fears, my insecurities, my anxieties, and my "acceptable" sins. It's crushed my pride. It's made me love deeper, forgive quicker, and prayer more fervently.

There are lessons everywhere in everything – even the hard stuff. If we will lean in, stay teachable, keep our heart open—He will show us His ways, His heart, His plans. He will bring beauty from what's broken, delight from a dandelion, fruit from thorns.

So, Jesus, yes…yes to the easy lessons and the hard ones. Yes, to the carving, the shaping, the growing. Yes, to You…forever and always. Our hearts say, "Yes."

Chapter 12...
Yes to Looking Up & Letting Go

They never prepared me for this – the ache that seeps into every hollow place where a memory should be. My boys are getting older now. Talking about leaving, planning for careers, dreaming of homes they will own and sweethearts they will marry. With each new conversation, my heart breaks a little. Alongside the joy of watching them find their courage and step up to the edge of the nest in preparations to fly away, there comes a deep sorrow for the years I will never have with them. Memories we will never share.

There were years we lost at the beginning that we will never find. They weren't ours to have. I know this and I have been okay with this…until now. The few years that we have had together simply seem…not enough. Not for my heart. Not for my arms. Putting on a brave face, I listen to their dreams. I cheer them on as they begin to stretch their wings. Oh, how I wish they weren't so ready to fly.

They don't need me as much now. I am no longer their only confidant. The boys that once found their courage holding onto my hand, now open the door for me. They carry my bags and fill my tank with gas. They prepare their own lunches and spend their own money. And, even though they are everything that a mom could hope for in her sons, my heart screams, "We should have more time! I'm not ready for all of this!" Other moms get eighteen years – a truth that is not lost on me. Unwept tears sting the backs of my eyes as I watch them wobble and flap and learn to fly. I want to protect them, shelter them under my wings for just a little longer.

Whether I'm ready or not, I'm no longer feeding newly hatched babies. I'm raising fledglings. I must embrace this season of parenting teenagers…even if I stumble through it like a calf learning to walk.

Rarely do I know what to say or how to say it. Rarely do I hit on the perfect mixture of holding on and letting go. Rarely do my attempts at being the "cool mom" pan out successfully. I have needed as much grace as I have given. I have learned more lessons from them than I have taught. Pressing through my grief for what we did not have, I see now that the same amount of courage needed for each bird to jump from the nest is also needed from each Mama bird to let them.

I wish I had known that. I wish someone had told me how devastating AND beautiful this season of life really is. It takes guts. There is a certain audacity, fierceness, and supernatural strength of will that must hold us together as we hold onto them less.

Moses' mother had it. Placing her son in a homemade basket, she set him upon a river teaming with alligators, hippos, and a large assortment of other wild things. This river was the main "life source" to the Egyptians was filled with boats large enough to smash a small basket into smithereens. It was a hectic highway for traders, a wild life habitat, the bathtub of an entire nation, and the irrigation system for all of Egypt's farmland. What she did was audacious. What she did was the very definition of brave. Walking down to the Nile, knowing all that she knew, she went into river, set down her baby in his basket, released her hold, and walked away.

This is part of motherhood, a part not often talked about. We often paint Moses' mother in children's book standing beside the river smiling as Moses' basket drifts out of sight. We picture her there, at peace, at rest, as she watches him float farther and farther away from her grasp. But what if she wasn't? What if she wept? What if she, like so many of us, struggled to take her hands off the basket and say yes to letting go?

Not long ago, I loved a boy. I loved him with every fiber of my being. I still do. Not a day goes by that I don't think of him, pray for him, wish that he was here with me. In the quiet of a sleeping house, I am too often found tear-stained, clutching a pillow, asking God why it didn't work, why it had to be this way, why He said no, why I had to let go.

Everyone else has moved on. I can't. My heart won't. I still see him in my mind—his rich chocolate skin, that dimple that always told me mischief and fun were around the corner, his laugh that filled up an entire room. Everywhere I look, I see a memory of our visits, our moments together, as we both attempted to find our way—I as his mother, he as my son.

This is the OTHER side of adoption. The side I had hoped I would never have to see. Yet, here I am, nursing deep wounds, weeping over memories made—some beautiful, some broken. This is failed adoption. It is a miscarriage of the heart and I'm learning it's okay to grieve it.

I had so many plans, so many dreams for him, for us. Looking forward hurts now in a way it never has before. I look forward into a future without him, a future I never expected. Adoption is supposed to be forever. The papers were ready to be filed. We were so close. My heart had chosen. My love had been given. And now, here I am tonight staring at a picture on my phone that I can't bring myself to delete, leaning how to say "yes" even when that means letting go.

Somebody needs to tell this story. Someone needs to use their voice. There is light at the end of the tunnel. The Homans are making it. We are going to be okay. You will too.

A few years ago, we took the children to the shores of Lake Huron for Mother's Day. As we walked along the beach, sand squishing between our toes, giggles of delighted children riding upon the wind, we stumbled upon a lighthouse. We were all mesmerized by it but none more than our youngest, Jedediah. He stood looking up at the lighthouse long after the others had lost interest and found their way back to the beach. He just couldn't take his eyes off it.

Running to the side of the lighthouse, he touched the cool brick, tracing the outline of the mortar with his finger, never taking his eyes from the top. Then, running back to where I sat on the wall around it, he sat next to me and stared in silent wonder. This repeated a number of times—touch the brick, sit in wonder, touch the brick, sit in wonder, and then finally, he spoke.

"I ain't never seen lighthouse before, Mama. It's so big, bigger than me. I ain't never seen a lighthouse before."

When he finally drew his eyes away from the top of the lighthouse and looked at me, as if signaling he had taken it all in and was ready to move on, the smile that spread across his face could have melted the hardest of hearts. In his face was nothing of the fearful boy I had met just months before...instead, all that could be seen, was childhood delight. Peeling my eyes off of his smile (which was no easy feat), I turned my attention to the lighthouse again and we sat there, just the two of us, looking up.

In 1913, this lighthouse faced a great storm. For days, the storm now known as the "White Hurricane" crashed into its brick walls. By the end, nineteen ships were destroyed and nineteen other ships were stranded. In the lighthouse, weathering it all, was a man by the name of Captain Frank Kimball. He once said, *"I watched waves as high as 30 to 40 feet pounding the Light Station, and I think if the storm had lasted another hour the Light Station would have been wiped out."*

This is how I have felt over the past months...like one more hour of this storm might wipe us out, unsure if I can make it through one more round of waves, wondering if the walls of my heart can endure one more blow.

But it was when Peter looked up at Jesus that he discovered he could walk on water. And THIS is how we have learned to survive the storm. We have learned the art of looking up even when it hurts, even when we don't understand, even when we can barely breathe from the pain. When the grief threatens to swallow us, we look up. When the memories haunt us and steal away our sleep, we look up. When the tears won't stop, we look up. When we look up, we see a the "Son of Righteousness rising with healing in his wings" (Malachi 4:2).

The lighthouse that Captain Frank was unsure would make it through the White Hurricane of 1913, now stands tall as a historical landmark along the Lake Huron. It still lights the way for many a ship that pass along the waters between the United States and Canada. What he thought would destroy it, has become only a part of its story.

"When you pass through the waters, I will be with you; And through the rivers, they will not overflow you. When you walk through the fire, you will not be scorched, Nor will the flame burn you (Isaiah 43:2).

When I began this journey, I looked at motherhood through rose-colored glasses. After sixteen years of storms and seasons, babies and teens, I have come to the conclusion that motherhood is very different than I once thought it was. The glasses are off and my eyes can now see clearly. Here, in this place called motherhood, beauty walks alongside brokenness, the breath taking and the heart breaking coincide. Here there is belly-aching laughter and there is also deep, soul-groans of grief. Loss and gain, letting go and holding on – all have a place here in this story. It is the best and the hardest thing I have ever done. And that's okay. It's all part of what makes motherhood, motherhood.

Moses' mother did what had to be done for her son realizing that when she set him upon the water, she wasn't trusting the Nile to keep him safe. She was trusting God. It was this trust in God—this looking up to the One who is overseeing it all—that gave her the courage to walk away. And it will be in trusting God that we will find the courage to take our hands off the basket and let God take control. Even if it hurts. Even if there is pain. Even if it means…letting go.

Chapter 13...
Yes to Deep-Seeded Joy

    The breeze blew gently across my face as I swayed in the hammock. The sun was shining, the birds were singing, the coffee was lukewarm, and the kids were playing happily. I looked up into the emerald leaves of the maple tree that held me secure and breathed out three simple words, "Joy lives here," and I meant them with every fiber of my being. In all of the chaos, in all of the noise, in all of the mess – there is JOY.

    People often say, "You're crazy." I have learned to respond, "Yes, I am. Crazy blessed." This life I live – it's a good one. Easy? No way. Exhausting? Sometimes. But joy-filled? ALWAYS. No one can make me laugh like my husband and kids can. They have unearthed sounds in me I never knew I could make. Like the "Squeal and Snort" and the "Smoker's Cough." Who knew my lungs were capable of such monstrosities? Who knew that joy could be felt all the way down to your toes? I didn't…until God gave me them.

They fill each day with a million reasons to say, "Thank you." A wiggle of an eyebrow at the perfect moment, a pun when you least expect it, an unplanned dance party in the Oatmeal aisle of Wal-Mart. All it takes is one of these moments and I am a goner. Laughter and gratitude are guaranteed to follow.

A few weeks ago, as we hurried to dress and feed our children for Wednesday Bible Study, our son, Gideon, decided that he could not be satisfied by simply wearing his "church best" to class. After refusing everything in his closet, he donned his white dress-up tuxedo with tails and bowtie, laced up his black tennis shoes, and drenched his hair in a bath of water and gel. Marching up the stairs proudly, he began walking back and forth in front of me like a peacock showing off his beautiful plumage in an effort to attract attention.

"Ma, what do you think? I think I look real good. Actually, I *know* I look real good."

Lifting my concentration from the braid, half-done in my hands, I looked at him slightly shocked and very much unsure of how to proceed. On the one hand, he was adorable. On the other hand, the outfit was a bit impractical.

"Wow! That is fun. But, uh, I don't think you need to be that dressy for church."

"Oh, Ma," he sighed. "I really want to wear this. I feel so nice."

"Okay," I responded, pausing only a moment to confirm my decision with my heart. "Why not? Go for it, kid. At least it's clean."

"Yes!" he celebrated, fist repeatedly pumping the air. "This is going to be great."

"Yes!" I agreed. "This IS great."

That night, as Gideon proudly walked the hallways of the church to his class, every single person who saw him smiled. They smiled! Not out of pity. Not out of politeness. They sent him true, genuine, wrinkle-your-eyes kind of smiles because his delight was contagious, because his joy set off joy in them—and he loved it. He ate it all up. He relished in it.

Then, the next week, when it came time to choose an outfit, you can bet your bottom dollar that he came back up those stairs with that darn tuxedo again and a huge, toothy grin.

"Hey, Ma…"

Children. They have a way of birthing joy and wonder in us. They see the world differently than we do. They don't need an all-inclusive beach vacation to find joy. They know exactly where it lives. In the splash of a mud puddle, in an intense game of Jenga, in a sticky marshmallow around a simple bon fire pit, in a dress-up tuxedo. They don't have to look far or do much to discover its whereabouts. They know what we often forget, that joy lives here and is available to us if we will simply reach out and lay hold of it.

Even on the hard days, it is visible. It is present. Joy doesn't rise and fall on the back of our circumstances. It is a constant companion and can be found at any time, by those who choose to seek it out.

Our son, Jordan, is one such "seeker of joy." We can be having the worst of days and he will find the perfect pun and share it at just the right time to bring us all to a place of eye-watering, belly-aching laughter. His comedy routines are a thing of beauty…and he knows it. The laughter he finds at the end of each of his jokes makes it even more enjoyable. Life is better with him in it.

Our daughter, Shiloh, does it too. "Mom, you sit down and we are going to put on a show for you." Her shows bring so much delight. I don't care what kind of day you are having, when you see a Chihuahua dressed up as a camel bringing gifts to baby Jesus and six-year old little brother swaddled in a large throw blanket being carried by Mother Mary (played by his ten year old sister who can barely hold him since they are almost the exact same size) – you will smile. It is impossible NOT to smile.

This is a good life. Joy has etched its name into so many of our memories, so many of our moments. I will forever look back on these days together as some of the best days of my life here on earth. Saying "yes" to God is the best thing we have ever done. Never will you hear us regret it. Never will you hear us wish we had chosen another path. Our "yes" opened the door to the grandest and most exciting of adventures. Our "yes" led us to a place of incredible joy. Our "yes" gave us: Reuben, Abraham, Peter, Jordan, Nevaeh, Shiloh, Brionna, Daniel, Isaiah, Hadassah, Ezekiel, Gideon, Phoebe, and Jedediah – fourteen living proofs that saying "yes" to God is most definitely and undeniably….worth it.

Saying "yes" to God is the best decision you will ever make.

After our last adoption, there was one particular day where it was as if my children couldn't get close enough to Mama. EVERYONE wanted to snuggle in. EVERYONE wanted my attention. Everything in our lives was changing – GOOD change, AWESOME change, but…CHANGE—and Mama-Cuddles made it all seem safer.

By the time my husband returned from work, I had a child in both arms, two holding my hands, two laying on my legs, one leaning against me, and three doing my hair. I was a mess, but they were at peace. As they braided and knotted my hair, rubbed their tiny hands up and down my arm, and touched my face for the millionth time, I was reminded of how God wants to use EVERY part of His body to express His love and reveal His glory in the earth just like every part of mine was being used to minister to my children. No, I did not have ten arms (which would seem the most logical choice), but that day, even the smallest strands of my hair had purpose – and that was enough. That was, to them, everything.

I often hear mothers compare themselves to me. "I don't know how you do it," they will say with an air of awestruck bewilderment laced with utter discouragement. They think I don't hear it, but I do. It drips liberally from their lips as they comment on how I was able to arrive on time with fifteen children and they can't get anywhere on time with only one child. It wraps like a blanket around their shoulders as they watch my children help me shop for groceries in a crowded store. "How can she do it and I can't?"

The answer is simple: Because I was made for this. Just like you were made and perfectly designed for what YOU are called to do.

Years ago, I babysat for one child. ONE child. By the end of the day, I was utterly exhausted. Being in charge of ONE child is so much work. My kids go out and play together for hours…this child wanted my undivided attention the entire day. How do parents of one child get any work done? It's amazing. I'm in awe. Mothers of one child – YOU ARE INCREDIBLE.

Comparison robs us of joy.

Did you hear me? Let me say that again, because that truth carries the power to set some of us free, today. Comparison robs us of joy!

We don't need others to make us feel small. We do that ourselves. We look to others and think, "She is so much better than I am." We wonder why we weren't blessed with those genes, those ninja skills, those vocal chops. We forget that every part of the body is needed, significant, and made with a purpose, we forget the absence of even the smallest parts will be felt and in doing so, we belittle ourselves. And in doing that, we belittle God. The God who made us, shaped us, and PLANNED us. The God who breathed stars into the sky and breath into our lungs. By looking down at ourselves, we downplay His creativity and holiness. And this is exactly what Satan wants.

If he can make us feel small, he can keep us from doing what God created us to do. Insecurity breeds timidity. It is the birth place of fear – fear of man, fear of rejection, fear of failure. It stifles. It suffocates. It smothers. This has always been the enemy's plan.

John 10:10 says that the thief comes to "steal, kill, and destroy." Exodus 1 tells us that it was Pharaoh's fear that motivated him to enslave the Israelite people. He knew that if they were to every fully recognize who they were, they could easily rally and take his kingdom. My friends, the enemy fights those he fears. He will do everything within his power to make you feel small, insignificant and unimportant because as long as you question your value, you won't say "Yes" to what God has called you to do on the earth.

Psalm 139:13-14 says this, **"For you formed my inward parts; you knitted me (You have intricately woven me) together in my mother's womb. I praise you, for I am fearfully and wonderfully (distinctly, separately) made.**

No one can take your place, my friend. You are one of a kind, distinct, rare, made from your own individual mold. You are not here by accident. He is the one who formed you, intricately weaving together every detail of who you are.

The Psalmist goes on to write this, in Psalm 139:14-16, **"Wonderful (distinct and special) are your works; my soul knows it very well (Because I am one of them!). My frame (substance, the very bones of who I am) was not hidden (concealed) from you, when I was being made in secret, intricately woven (embroidered, skillfully sewn, mixed with color) in the depths of the earth. [16] Your eyes saw my unformed substance; in your book were written, every one of them, the days that were formed for me (from my conception to my death), when as yet there was none of them."**

The hands of God skillfully sewed every detail of who you are together. You may have surprised your parents upon your arrival, but you were not a surprise to God. You were a part of His plan, His story from the beginning. It was His hands that formed and shaped you and His breath that brought you to life! He said "yes" to you!

You were made on purpose for a purpose. Walk confidently in that truth.. The first step in living your "yes" for God is saying "no." No to insecurity. No to fear. No to comparison. No to any voice that tells you that you are less than or insignificant. When you say "no" to those voices, God's voice will become clearer. And as you follow His voice, He will lead you into abundant life!

Chapter 14...
Yes to Giving Him Your Basket

As a mother of nine boys and five girls, I have begun to compile a list of things I never thought I'd ever say. The list is endless—growing every single day, right alongside my children.

Here are just a few of my favorites:

Who flushed the "my little pony" down the toilet?

Why is their underwear hanging from my tree?

No, you may not climb on the roof with your homemade parachute and jump off.

No, frogs do not count as visitors for church.

Who let the lizards out tonight?

Child, why are you wearing your pants on your head?

And my all-time favorite: *"Who painted the cat green?"*

This was said in response to an epic Pinterest-fail. "Snow Paint" they called it. They had promised it would keep my children entertained for hours. I don't know who "they" are, but I want to publicly inform them that they are horribly wrong. Arming my children with enough snow paint to rainbow-print every inch of our ten acres and directing them towards the door, I breathed deeply of ten seconds of quiet. In the middle of a Michigan winter when most of your roommates smell like puberty – ten seconds of quiet is pretty much an angelic visitation.

Before I knew it, they were on their way back inside and I was looking out the window to see their handiwork. Puzzled, I asked, "Kids, why is the snow still white? Where did the paint go?"

Before they could speak, I had my answer. Coming from around the corner of the house and into my line of sight, came our good ole kitty, Miracle. No longer speckled white and grey, she strutted towards the house with a brand new coat… of many colors. At least it was non-toxic.

Sigh.

If there was a "Most Unlikely To Have Fourteen Kids" category, I'd be one of the names on the top of the list.

Here's just a few reasons why:

1. I'm easily overwhelmed in crowds and thrive on quiet time.

2. I like a neat and orderly home where everything has its place (mind you, my husband would say I like "organized chaos" – something he believes is a far cry from neat and orderly. To each his own).
3. I hate rodents, snakes, lizards, and every other creepy crawly my boys decide to name "pet."
4. I have a serious lack of patience at times.
5. My hair abilities begin and end at pony tail.
6. I like sleep…like LOVE it. If sleeping were an Olympic Sport, I'd medal. There are few things in this world that I love more than the feeling of my soft, warm blanket wrapped around me as my pillow gently cushions my head.
7. I do not like all the "common children-friendly" meal options. Chicken Nuggets, Hot Dogs. Get thee behind me, Satan.
8. And, at the very top of the list, of why I should not be the mother of so many children, I absolutely hate, loathe, detest, and disdain… laundry. It is the thorn in my side, the bee in my bonnet, the hair on my plate.

Oh, and, number nine, I have no idea how to get green paint out of cat fur.

And this is only the short list!

Sure, I could tackle one or two, maybe even four or five kids…but fourteen? No, this was not my plan. This is not something I am qualified for nor am capable of. But God. He's the wild card, the wrench, the game changer. He loves using the most unlikely. He has a special place in his heart for the under-achiever, the benched. **He loves to put us in situations where the outcome can only be explained by**

pointing upward. To use our lives in such a way that the only response is to give Him all the glory because it just couldn't be us. It's just not possible without Him. **And this is how I feel every single day.**

I live fully aware of my inability, fully aware that I'm not cut out for this on my own, but also fully aware that I can do all things through Christ. He is what qualifies me and that reality sets me on the edge of my seat. It makes my heart explode with expectation and excitement. It shatters all the boundaries I place around my life, all the limits I feel safe to dream within. If what God can do through my life is based on HIS ABILITIES and not my own, then there are NO limits to what He can do!

Luke 18:27 says that "what is impossible for man is possible for God."

Living a "yes" for God will often require us to dream beyond our limits and to embrace the ground outside our comfort zones. It will call us to step beyond what makes sense in the natural and reach for things that may even feel a bit unrealistic. Some may even call them impossible. Oh, how our God LOVES the impossible. **He is in the business of taking inadequate offerings and using them to meet impossible needs.** Take the feeding of the five thousand in John 6 as a perfect example.

Five loaves and two fish in MY home would be an appetizer. The offering—this little boy's lunch basket—was completely inadequate. There was no possible way to feed five men, let alone five thousand from this simple lunch. It just wasn't enough. It would never be enough. Looking at it, the disciples asked the obvious questions.

"But what it this when there are so many?"

How often I have asked that same question? How often have I looked down into my own basket, insecure about what I have to give and wondered how God could ever use this simple offering?

I have become very good at comparing myself with others. All humans tend to gold medal in this Olympic sport. Be the best, look the best, write the best status, calligraphy the best invitation, cook the best heart-healthy meal, exercise the best or feel the worst because you don't measure up. Instagram, Facebook, and Pinterest have fed into this spirit of comparison that has captivated and crippled the body of Christ. We look into each other's baskets and always feel we come up short – my offering seeming so much less than yours.

"Look at what she has to offer. She can sing and dance and chase a toddler in stilettos. I trip over my house slippers."

"Ugh. She is exercising again!? How does she have time? She is so fit. I bet she doesn't even wear spanks."

"How is it possible he got another promotion? Now he has all this money. I bet he even has a boat."

We'd love to blame all of this insecurity and comparison on social media, but the truth is it feeds what has always been there. This has been one of humanities struggles from the very beginning and is found woven throughout the Bible's vibrant tapestry of historical accounts again and again and again. Since the Garden of Eden, the enemy has done all that can do to make us feel small and less than. Why? Because he knows if he can make us question what we carry, we will never give it to God to use.

I'm writing that out again, because I need you to hear it. The WORLD needs you to hear it: **The enemy knows that if he can make you question what you carry, you will never give it to God to use**. "And who knows, but that you were brought to the kingdom for SUCH A TIME AS THIS?!" (Esther 4:14)

Shiloh, my daughter, is a beautiful, kind, creative soul. She is everything I wish I would have been and think I could have been at the age of twelve had it not been for my intense struggle with insecurity. I watch her dance wildly, laugh loudly, join in conversations and I'm in awe of her bravery. She is sugar and spice and courage and love all rolled into one. I am amazed by her and what she carries. I look at her as she sews costumes for her little siblings and writes songs on a notepad secretly tucked underneath her bed, and I think, "This girl has something special."

My son, Isaiah, is handsome and strong, built like an ox, athletic and wild. Not only can he scale walls (like…literally, scale them) and run miles without breaking a sweat, he can also draw and paint the most beautiful pictures I have ever seen. I look at him and I just know, "This boy has something special."

And it's not just them – it's all of fourteen of them. Jordan and his quiet strength and hilarious sense of humor; Abraham with his intellectual conversations and musical stylings; Reuben with his incredibly kind heart and strength of will; Brionna with her determination and fearless resolve; Peter with his creative and inventive mind; Nevaeh with her gentle love; Daniel and his infectious joy; Phoebe's fearless and tenacious take on life; Hadassah's open heart; Ezekiel's quiet strength; Gideon's joy and passion for life;

Jedediah's wisdom way beyond his years – I look at them and I say, "These kids – they have something special." I can see it in them. I can see what they carry. **And the way that I look at them, the Father is looking at you.** There is something special in you – something HE put there that HE wants to use. To you, it may not look like much, but in His hands – five surrendered loaves of bread and two fish can feed multitudes!

That's why I love this story in John 6. It proves that when we give God what we have, **our little become much in his hands**. By the end of the story, not only was everyone fed, there were also twelve baskets full of leftovers. Jesus did "exceedingly, abundantly more" than was necessary. He did the impossible. Using one little boy's lunch, He fed a multitude.

I wonder – what could He do with your basket? With mine? What would happen if you worried less about measuring up to others and more about lifting up what we have to Him? What could He do with a people like that? With a people who lived a "Yes?"

A few years ago, my husband and I were asked to speak for an award ceremony where we would be receiving an award for our service as foster and adoptive parents. Looking out across the many faces that had gathered, we felt foolish. We felt like imposters. *Why were we here?* We hadn't done anything special. We just loved our kids. And then, it hit me – *"Niki, God has given you a platform tonight. Use it."*

So we did...and every other one that He has placed us on. Are we qualified? No way. Is it still unreal all the doors God has opened, people we have rubbed shoulders with, and platforms we have stood upon to share our story? Absolutely. I didn't finish college! I have no real training, no education or study to back what I say. I just have my stories. And as I lift them up for Him to use – He takes my small basket and feeds multitudes.

I am okay with the fact that I will never be qualified for this life. I fully accept that my offering will always be inadequate. I will never have what it takes in and of myself. Yet, that's the beauty of it all! As I just give Him my basket, He takes it and uses it for His glory and He does things I could never imagine and takes me places I never thought I would see. He does the impossible through me as I simply say, "Yes" to Him.

So, what gifts, talents, and resources has He placed in your hands? Are you a cook? God can use that. Are you an artist? God can use that too. Are you a letter writer? A scrapbooker? A card player? Do you ride a skateboard? Do you like going out to eat on Sunday after church? Can you build stuff or change the oil in a car or are you just really good at showing up? God can use all of that. Just give it to Him, give Him your "YES!" and see what He can do!

Epilogue

"This is our moment," my husband whispers in my ear as he gently pulls me by the hand towards the house. Reaching in to his pocket, he stealthily pulls out a wad of water balloons he had confiscated from the kids bucket and winks at me.

"They won't even know what hit them."

After taking one last look at the children playing in the yard, we quietly ducked into the house and tiptoed into the kitchen, stifling our giggles, as we made plans and filled balloons.

"We are going to get them this time! If I go around the this side of the house and you go around that side of the house," my husband strategized as his hands moved quickly through the air. All of our years of parenting had led us to this moment and we knew it. The children had always won these battles. But not today. Not in this house. Today…it was our turn.

Within minutes, we tiptoed back to the door holding our mixing bowls full of balloons and feeling rather proud of ourselves.

"Ready?" my husband asked as he opened the door.

"Ready!" I responded.

"3…2…1…WATER FIGHT!"

Funny thing about that water fight. The kids weren't actually surprised we were coming. In fact, the whole time we had been inside filling balloons and preparing our strategy, they had been outside doing the same. And I would like to say we bravely held our ground and valiantly refused to run from the field of battle. However, this was not the case. By the end, Matthew and I looked less like 30-something-year-old parents and more like two cats who had been dumped in a bucket of water. We had lost. Fourteen children verse two parents is hardly a fair fight. But it was a fun one we will never forget.

I have battled with what to say as I end this book, because our story is so far from over. How do you end what has yet to end? How do you bring closure to a story that He is still writing? The truth is: you can't. And I'm kind of okay with that, because if parenting has taught me anything at all, it has taught me that life, like motherhood, is just one giant, grand adventure – less about a destination and more about the journey. And that some of our best moments await us just beyond our "Yes." Oh, friend…say, "Yes" to Jesus and just see what He will do.

Much love,

A Very Wet Mama Bear

About the Author

Nicole Homan is an author, speaker, worship leader, songwriter and the founder of Planted – a ministry designed to encourage and equip women to "display His glory" wherever God has planted them. She has authored two books, recorded multiple albums, and is currently working on a number of devotionals for women.

Nicole and her family live in Michigan, where they have pastored for many years. Her children, at the time of this book's publication, range in age from 8 to 18. There is never a dull moment in the Homan household.

For more information or to discuss scheduling Nicole Homan for your next event, email: nicolemhoman@gmail.com.

Made in the USA
Monee, IL
01 May 2021